LEADERSHIP & GOLF:

Creating Organizational Alignment

by

Thomas K. Wentz &
William S. Wentz

ORDERING INFORMATION

LEADERSHIP & GOLF may be purchased for educational, business, or sales promotional use. For information please write:

Corporate Performance Systems, Inc.
5001 Pine Creek Drive
Westerville, Ohio 43081
Tel: (614) 890-2799 Fax: (614) 890-6760

or visit our web sites at:
www.swingtobalance.com
www.transchange.com

Cover design by Janet Loper, Boehm, Inc.

The paper used in this publication meets the requirements of the American National Standard for Permanence of Paper for Printed Library Materials Z39.49-1984.

Library of Congress Control Number: 2002090404

LEADERSHIP & GOLF: Creating Organizational Alignment
    by Thomas K. Wentz and William S. Wentz– 1st ed.

ISBN 0-9668435-1-7

*This book is dedicated to Nancy, the Center of Gravity of our lives.
Every person must have both static and dynamic balance in their lives.
The absolute key is to know that the Center of Gravity is a constant
source of inspiration and support.*

*For us that has been Nancy, our wife and mother respectively.
Thank you for your love and support.*

Tom and Bill

Table of Contents

Table of Contents - Continued

INTRODUCTION

This book is about 16 managers who need to change, want to change, have tried to change and have been *handicapped* by the commands coming from their company's senior executives. The company began losing market share two years ago and everyone is aware that change is essential. Their intentions are good. They know that the key ingredients are leadership and teamwork. Yet, they have been unable to translate their intentions into reality.

As the book reveals, the CEO uses the command "Make it happen." The chairman is demanding more with less. The vice president of Sales is telling his people to hit the numbers and work smarter not harder. The vice president of Operations isn't sure what to tell his people other than to be a team. The frustration within the organization has turned to conflict and blame. Customers are asking for the impossible and the customer service manager is caught in the middle of the battle between Engineering, Operations, and Sales.

This organizational situation is very similar to the experience of many golfers. Most players want to improve their game. They have tried many ways to change their game. They spend a fortune on exotic golf schools, constantly watch the Golf Channel searching for the magic idea, try every tip in the golf magazines, buy new clubs, and remain in a *handicapped* state that doesn't improve. They have convenient excuses of time and talent and accept their handicapped condition as the way it is.

The story that unfolds in this book originates from our Business Simulation entitled Swing to Balance: Creating Organizational Alignment. It is a story about leadership and achieving your potential. It is about organizational excellence in whatever form you are currently seeking it. It is about commitment to a team and mastery of personal emotions.

The need for great coaches and leaders has never been more apparent than it is today. The profile of the great coach has changed. The charismatic, confrontational, heroic models of the past have been replaced with a focused, confident, enrolling, and disciplined style. As modeled in this book, leaders today must be able to transform the *muscle memory* that prevents the organization from changing This transformation must be made with alignment and commitment, not compliance, from the entire organization. It will surprise you how simple it is.

All the people in the story and their experiences during the Swing to Balance Simulation are real. Their names have been changed and their stories have been combined to provide maximum meaning to their experiences during and following the Simulation.

Some characters in the book hate golf and others have never played the game before. To them the language and rules of golf are totally foreign. The same is true in business. We work with executives every day who hate competing in the new business environment. They give the new game lip service but continue to manage by the old rules. They don't understand the language of the new game and are frustrated by having to empower people.

I am confident you will relate to at least one of the characters. My friends who read the manuscript universally said they quickly related with the dilemma of a specific character as being much like their own business experience.

For those of you who hate golf, I suggest that you put yourself in Ariel's shoes. She hates golf, is required to participate, and in the end makes an enormous contribution to her team. The lesson she learns may be important to your life as well.

If you have had a bad experience on the golf course with a husband, father, or other pseudoinstructor, you will appreciate the plight of Tina who quit golf years ago because it almost ruined her marriage. Get in the cart with Tina and experience the transformation that she experiences on the ninth hole.

If no one listens to your ideas at work, yet you think you are smarter than the boss, try to understand Wally as he plays his old game. Realize how important it is to be a master of influence and how his old game just doesn't get his message through.

If you are an avid golfer and would love to improve, you will enjoy Al's story. Al learns to change his game from *hitting balls* to *Swinging to Balance*. Al is fascinated by this simple command and finally understands how to translate it into a powerful concept on the course and at work.

If you know an executive with a big ego, you will see that person in Ron. You will realize that Ron has an addiction that is masked by his phony bravado and intimidating style. If you must work with a person like Ron, read the book to find out how he realizes he is a part of the team. The transformation of the heroic manager model is the single biggest challenge in business today.

If you are a financial person and have difficulty comprehending the link between the bottom line and organizational culture, you will learn from the experiences of Jill and Cheryl. The leverage for economic performance in the story is startling.

All the characters are challenged by the process of transforming the *muscle memory* of their old game so their team can be successful. The emotional learning revealed in the story is a powerful process.

As always, it would be impossible to thank all the people who made this book possible. To the participants of the Swing to Balance Simulation, we thank you for participating. It is easier to quit or not attend than to play a game as frustrating as golf. Our thanks to our many students like Al. They inspired us to record the victory over the muscle memory of the old swing and the old way of doing business. It is a constant battle.

We especially want to thank those who have used the Swing to Balance concept to transform the way they think and act at home and in business. The vivid memories of how you were emotionally confronted with your old game will always be remembered.

Many thanks to all the people who took time to read the manuscripts and give feedback on the flow of the story. All the input was valuable in making the book more interesting and easy to read.

Finally we want to give special thanks to all the professional golfers who have committed their lives to one simple concept—Swing to Balance. The pursuit of balance sounds too simple to be a powerful context for living and working. However, the end of a perfect swing is always in balance. The same is true in business and life.

William (Bill) S. Wentz
Golf Professional and
Vice President Golf Operations

Thomas (Tom) K. Wentz
President

Chapter 1
Frustrated with the Old Game

"Hi Al, how's your game?"

"Terrible!"

"What brings you out on a nasty day like this?"

"I'm going to a strategic planning conference in Florida next week and I thought I'd try one more time to figure out how to hit this thing."

"What thing?"

"This new driver and all the other *things* for that matter. I haven't played well all year. Actually, I resigned from the club. I'm not going to put myself through this agony any more. I'm not sure which is worse, golf or my job."

It was Sunday afternoon in late October. About fifty degrees and windy. Nobody was on the driving range except Al and I. I was headed to Hilton Head the next week to give a speech and wanted to work on my swing. Al was obviously here in desperation trying to figure out the problem with his game.

"I saw you taking a lesson from Gary several months ago. Did that help?" I asked.

"No. I couldn't do what he wanted me to do. He told me to change my grip and narrow my stance. I started to shank everything."

"I've been watching you and can see what you're doing wrong. Would you like me to help you?"

I had been watching Al for twenty minutes and could see that he has what I call the lawn mower swing. In an attempt to keep the right elbow connected to their right side, many players drag the right elbow around behind their body as if they were pulling the starter cord on a lawn mower.

"I'm not sure anything can help me. I've tried everything that I've seen on the Golf Channel and nothing works," Al explained.

"I'd be glad to show you how to do it correctly."

"Is it that Swing to Balance stuff? I tried that when you gave me the video and it didn't help at all," Al said. "I would fall over every time I tried it."

I had given Al our golf video entitled Swing to Balance two years ago. The video illustrates the Balanced Finish position, and it is difficult to do in the beginning.

"It's like riding a bike. It takes time to learn to balance. Do you want me to show you how?" I asked.

"Do you think it would help?" he replied.

"We'll, based on your current condition it sure wouldn't hurt," I suggested.

I play with people who have all the excuses for their bad golf game. They don't have enough time to practice and they won't take lessons because it won't help. They'll try something once, and if it doesn't produce immediate results, they'll try something else. They experiment themselves into the hopeless state that Al was in.

"Let's give it a try," I said. "You're having problems because you're trying to *hit the ball* rather than *swing the club*. I'm going to teach you how to swing the club and let the club hit the ball. If you swing the club properly, it will do what it is designed to do."

"That sounds too simple," Al said.

"It is simple, but it is not easy," I confirmed. "Let's start at the end of the swing. The one thing that all professional golfers do is end up in a Balanced Finish position like this." I demonstrated the Balanced Finish position. "It's like business. The books must balance at the end of every month. Right?"

"Don't remind me of our business," Al cynically said. "We are so messed up right now. It's just like my golf swing."

"Golf swings and businesses both get messed up for the same reason. Efforts to hit the ball in golf are the same as efforts to hit the numbers in business. Both approaches lead to constant manipulation and sooner or later you will lose your sense of balance."

Al looked at me with a confirming look. Something about the word manipulation made a connection for him.

"I've tried everything. Sometimes, I feel so manipulated my body feels like a pretzel, and the sales guys are always manipulating us," Al said.

"There are many things about golf and business that are the same. You might be able to learn what I'm about to teach you if we relate it to business."

I put Al in the Balanced Finish position. "Feel your body in this position. I want you to be able to repeat this position every time you swing." As I held Al's body in the Balanced Finish position, I said, "The body is tall. The head is up looking down the fairway. The right shoulder is past the left. The right toe is straight up. If it was a nail you could drive it into the ground. You are standing on your left leg. The hands are beside your left ear and the club is behind you back."

"I've never been in this position before. Wow, this really feels strange. Are you sure this is right?" Al asked.

"They taught Tiger the balanced finish position when he was three years old. We have a picture of him in this position at the office. Yes, I know it's right and I know it feels strange. All changes in muscle memory positions feel strange at first, but it will become comfortable as you stretch your muscles. Try it again."

Al swung the club to Balance several times. At first, he could not hold his balance. "See I always fall over," he said. "This can't be right."

"I'll help you balance. Balance is not natural. It needs to be developed like a baby learning to walk," I suggested.

Al would swing and I would hold him in Balance after the swing. He was athletic so it didn't take long before he said, "I get it."

"Do it again. Good. Four more times." By now he was doing it without my support.

"That's easy. Why didn't Gary show me this?"

"All teaching professionals have their own method of teaching. You'd have to ask Gary?" I said.

"You're now ready for the next step. Want to go on?" I asked

"Sure, but can I try hitting a ball first?" he asked.

"Al, you must never say hit a ball again during this lesson. You swing the club. The club hits the ball. No, you aren't ready to swing at a ball yet. I'll let you swing at a ball after we have the whole Swing to Balance process installed in your muscle memory. Okay?"

"Sure. Let's keep going. What's next?" he asked.

"I now want you to swing to Balance Finish, then swing backward to the top of the back swing, then back to Balanced Finish. Let me show you." I demonstrated the process and said, "Do it about six times until it starts to feel fluid." I showed him the process and handed him the club.

Al began to swing the club back and forth in a complete swing. He had trouble balancing at first, but it started to work on the fifth swing.

"Do it easy. Can you feel yourself swinging the club?" I asked.

"Yes. I've never done this before. It feels so effortless."

"The golf swing is effortless. That's why you see those little guys hit it a long way," I said. "They swing the club with speed and Balance. That's why they are great players," I added.

"Let's move on," I suggested. "The next step is to put the club in the right position with your axis of rotation. To make it all work, the club must swing perpendicular to the axis of rotation. It is important to know that there are laws of physics that govern the golf swing. Just like in your business, there are laws of accounting that govern how you operate."

I showed Al the Balanced Set-up position. "You must be in an athletic position where your rear end is up and behind your body. Most players have their rear end under them." Once again, I demonstrated the position for him. "See how my arms hang straight down? My hands are inside my eyes. In this position my arms are relaxed. The leg muscles are flexed. In this position I could play quarterback, shortstop, or basketball. It is the same in all sports. The legs must be in control."

I helped Al assume the position. "Put the club across your body where your legs join your hip joints.—Now lock your knees back and stand tall from the waist up. Now, using the club push your rear end back and up and simultaneously lean your chest and head out over your toes.—Keep your back straight.—You'll feel tension in the small of your back.—Feel your body. Now let your knees flex without letting your rear end come under you. Great! Now drop your arms and grip the club.—Feel your body.—You're now in the Balanced Set-up position."

The biggest flaw in most amateur golf swings is a faulty Set-up. Everything proceeds down hill from a poor Set-up.

"Wow, this feels weird," Al said. "I've never been in this position before. Are you sure this is right?" he asked.

"It's right," I assured him. "Every position that is not in your current muscle memory will feel weird at first. Just feel your body in this position so you can repeat the process every time you set up. It will get comfortable the more you do it."

When he was in the Balance Set-up position, I said, "Freeze. Don't move. Hold the position you're in and note that the club is perpendicular to your spine. It is this relationship that is most important in swinging the golf club. The club must maintain that relationship for the ball to go straight," I said with some emphasis.

Once again, I held Al in the Balanced Set-up position for thirty seconds to program his muscle memory. "Now, I want you to swing to the Balanced Finish position we practiced earlier. Do you remember it?" I asked.

"Yeah," he nodded.

"Maintain your spine angle until the club is pointing down the fairway, then let the body go up to the Balanced Finish position. Got it?"

"Wow, that really feels strange!" he said. "But, it feels so effortless."

"Do it again. Start with the Balanced Set-up. Grip the club. Now swing up to Balance." I coached him through the process ten times.

"It's hard to hold the Balanced Finish position. I keep losing my balance," he said.

"It's like riding a bike. You'll get it in about ten more swings," I suggested.

"When are we going to hit some balls? I mean swing at some balls? Sorry," Al apologized.

"Don't be sorry. You don't need to apologize when you are learning new thoughts. The old ways of saying things aren't easily replaced," I laughed. "It's like business. Managers always tell their people to hit the numbers. They never say swing to balance."

"What?" Al asked.

"I teach some of my clients to use the Swing to Balance command at work. It is difficult for them to break the hit the numbers habit." I paused for a moment then said, "We'll swing at a ball as soon as you can Swing to Balance and hold the finish for five seconds. Keep swinging," I said.

"What about my grip? Gary said my grip was wrong," Al added.

"Your grip is already different because you hands are now inside your eyes at set-up. I can see that it has changed. But we'll adjust the grip once we see how the ball is going. Keep swinging. Swing to Balance. Swing to Balance. It's coming."

Al practiced swinging the club until he could balance. "It's starting to feel natural," he remarked.

"You're looking great. Ready to swing at a ball?"

"Yeah! Let's try it."

"Let me explain what will likely happen. When the ball appears, your brain will tell your right hand to hit the ball. If you think hit the ball, there is nothing in that command for your hands to do once they hit the ball. There will be a natural follow through by the hands because of momentum. But there is no conscious end to the swing in the hit the ball command. Does that make sense?" I asked.

"A hit the ball golf swing will always hit it crooked. It is not a matter of whether, just how bad will it be," I suggested.

"Remember when you played baseball?" I asked.

"Yes."

"After you hit the ball what did you do?"

"Dropped the bat and started running to first," Al said.

"Correct. You didn't Swing to Balance and watch the ball until it landed. Right?"

"Of course not," Al agreed.

"Many people who play golf use a baseball swing to hit the golf ball. That is the only command they have in their brain and the only way they know how to swing," I added. "It's the same in business. The command is hit the numbers and nothing else matters. Have you heard that command recently?"

"That's all we ever talk about. It's driving me crazy and that's all we'll hear at the planning retreat. Numbers! Numbers! Numbers!"

"Well, use your frustration with the numbers orientation at work to remind you not to do that on the golf course. The golf course is a place where you can get away from hit the numbers." I suggested.

"I get it. If I want to relax, I go to the golf course. Right?" Al said. "That's amazing. I've never thought about golf that way."

"That's because you've been programmed to hit the ball out here and it is as frustrating here as it is at work."

"Does that mean that we would be relaxed at work if we were programmed to Swing to Balance, whatever that means in business?" he asked.

"Absolutely. If an organization is integrated cross functionally to serve customers in an effortless and effective way, you would be relaxed at work."

I paused for a moment so that thought could sink in. I could see Al processing what I had said. I had to change his focus back to golf or I wouldn't get to work on my swing. "As you know, in golf we don't drop the club and run after we hit the ball. We must swing the club all the way to Balance Finish and hold it until the ball lands."

"Let's try it. But, I'm going to control the command center in your brain. When I say go, all you need to do is swing the club to Balance. Ready? Set-up. — Swing to Balance, Swing to Balance, Swing to Balance, Swing to Balance, Swing to Balance, Go!"

Al swung to Balance for the first time in his golf career and hit a beautiful straight shot.

"Wow! Look at that! That's amazing! I haven't hit one that well all year!"

"Let's do it again!" he said reaching for another ball.

"Okay. Set-up. Swing to Balance, Swing to Balance, Swing to Balance, Swing to Balance, Go!"

"Wow! Look at that! Right down the middle! This can't be true! Why do you keep yelling Swing to Balance at me like that?" he asked.

"So your brain can't think hit the ball. If you stand over the ball for two or three seconds, your command center will tell your right hand to hit the ball and it will not work. I will teach you to change the command yourself, but right now I need to help you get through the first ten swings. Then you will be on your own."

Al continued his newfound swing. After the tenth swing, I didn't control his command center and the result was a horrible slice.

"See! I knew it wouldn't last," he said.

"Why do you think that happened?"

"I don't know. What did you say to yourself before you swung?" I asked.

"Nothing, I guess," he said.

"That's probably true. Without me providing the command, your brain went back to the hit the ball command that it knows and loves," I added. "Your old command of hit the ball is still in your brain. It is not only in your brain, it's deeply imbedded in your muscle memory as well. Hit the ball is instinctive. It will take time to replace that command with Swing to Balance."

"How long will it take me to learn this?" he asked.

"You've already learned it intellectually. It will take at least a year to install it in your muscle memory," I said.

"A year! I have to play next week!" he shouted. "I can't wait a year."

"I'm sorry. That's why it is important to start young players out with the right fundamentals. If you go from baseball to golf, you're going to struggle for several years," I said.

"Your son Bill is a golf pro, right? When did you teach this to him?" he asked.

"Unfortunately, he played baseball until he was twelve. His golf coach suggested he give up baseball if he wanted to be a good golfer. He learned it when he was twelve, but it took him several years to defeat the baseball swing."

We continued to work with Al's new driver. This time, I controlled his command center on every other swing. In-between I told Al to think Swing to Balance on his own before starting to swing. It was amazing to watch. Thirty minutes ago he was ready to quit the game. He was now on fire with enthusiasm.

"Does this Swing to Balance stuff work with an iron?" he asked.

"Sure. The same swing works with the irons. You just start with the ball in a different position," I said.

"Let's try an iron," I suggested, handing him a five iron. "Set up. Move the ball to the middle of your stance. With an iron you must hit down on the ball." I repositioned the ball for him. He adjusted his stance. "Good. That's excellent. Keep your spine angle steady. Ready? Swing to Balance, Swing to Balance, Swing to Balance, Go!"

"Wow! Look at that! I can't believe it!" he exclaimed.

"It is amazing isn't it?" I said. "You may get this in less than a year," I laughed.

Al was pulsating with excitement. We spent another twenty minutes working on the process. Some shots were horrible, but every time he hit it bad, he was aware that the hit the ball impulse controlled his swing.

"You can now understand why some people do miracles on the driving range but can't get it to work on the golf course. When they are on the range, they accidentally get into a swing the club mode. On the range they don't have a distance command in their brain. They are just swinging. When they go to the first tee, the command changes. They think hit the ball and the old muscle memory takes over," I explained.

"That happens to me a lot. There are some days when I think I have it figured out on the range. Then I go to the course and the disaster happens. I told my wife I'm not going to do this to myself any more. That's why I resigned. Resigned! I don't need to do that now. I've got to go get that letter back. With this Swing to Balance thing I can play again."

"Relax Al. The Club office is closed today."

"Oh, that's right." He paused for a moment then asked. "Where did you learn this?"

"It's in all the golf magazines and on the Golf Channel every night. Actually, I played with Gary last week and he does it on every swing. You just need to know what you're looking at and build the right commands into your brain. It's like business."

"What does that mean?" Al asked.

"I've been reading about your company in the papers lately. The market has changed and the stockholders are angry. You're going on a strategic planning retreat to try and figure out how to hit the numbers. There is a big difference between the commands that leaders use and those used by managers. The manager command is hit the numbers. A leader would command the organization to Swing to Balance."

"You can say that again. All we hear is hit the numbers and shareholder value! And when we hit the numbers, it's never good enough. What does Swing to Balance mean in a company?" he asked.

"Al, that's a great question, but I need to work on my swing before next week. I'm giving a speech to a group of executives in Hilton Head about Swing to Balance as a leadership concept. We're going to play after the speech and my swing needs some work. I promised my wife I'd be home for dinner. Why don't we defer that conversation until later? Maybe we could meet sometime in the next two weeks and talk about your business problem."

"But I need the answer before our meeting next week. How can we do strategic planning without knowing what Swing to Balance means? I can't believe that I played all year without knowing what you taught me in the last hour. What a waste of time this year has been."

"I know Al. People play with a bad golf swing year after year. They practice the wrong swing over and over expecting it to get better. After a while they accept their handicapped swing. The same is true in business. Golf and leadership are the two most overtaught underlearned games in the world."

Hi, this is Al. I can't tell you how excited I was when I went home that night. My wife had heard me complain about my game all year. When I came home and everything had changed, she thought I was crazy. Do you know how difficult it is to tell someone about an experience you've had, that they didn't have, when they don't care? My wife is tried of my golf saga. She's heard me say, "I got it" a thousand times.

I showed her what I had learned. I was swinging in our family room and accidentally took a divot out of our carpet. I had never hit down on the ball before. My wife went crazy. I'll buy her new carpet. Maybe that will help her tolerate my new golf life.

I was confused but intrigued by what Tom had said about managers hit the numbers and leaders Swing to Balance. I wasn't sure what Swing to Balance meant in business, but I sure knew what hit the numbers means. The possibility of being relaxed at work is zero. That will never happen. We all went to a leadership seminar that suggested we should relax and work together. We were ready to try it when the orders came down to do more with less. We started to reengineer and that elevated the conflict and tension. I'm as tired of the hit the numbers game at work as I am with hit the ball on the golf course.

I found the Swing to Balance video Tom had given me two years earlier and started to show it to my wife. As I watched it, I could see the mistake I was making which Tom calls the lawn mower pull. It was so obvious because I knew what I was looking for.

The rest of this story is fascinating. I hope you have as much fun reading it as I did living it. I'll talk to you at the end of each chapter. See you then.

Chapter 2
The Correct Command

My speech in Hilton Head was entitled *Releasing Human Potential*. The audience was a group of CEOs who had identified the need to release human potential as the leverage point for changing the way that their companies operate.

During the speech, I told of my experience with Al. I asked for a show of hands from those who had had a similar experience with their golf game. Nearly everyone raised his or her hand. The question is "Why?" My presentation confirms that people fail to *release their potential* because senior leaders do not give them the proper commands. Using the golf metaphor, I suggested that most people at a driving range would tell you they are hitting balls. Professional golfers go to the driving range to work on their swing. It looks like the same activity, but the commands being executed are very different.

I asked the audience if they could recall the encouragement that Vijay Singh's son had given his father before the final round of the 2000 Masters? Vijay's son told him *"Trust your swing, daddy."* Vijay went on to win the tournament. His son could have said hit it good or hit it straight or hit it long. The universal golf command is trust your swing.

"How about a chip shot?" someone asked. "Don't you just hit a chip?"

This question opened up the discussion about swinging and hitting even on short shots. "Since much of golf is about feel and instinct, it is difficult to say that all shots are swings not hits," I suggested, "You need to do both. The same is true in business. Every company must Swing to Balance by serving customers AND hit the numbers." I suggested that they knew the concept as win-win.

I had been home three days when my phone rang. "Hello.—Hi Al, what's going well?" I asked.

"What's going well? What kind of a question is that?" he asked.

"We want things to go well every day, don't we?" I asked. "It would be an awful day if something wasn't going well," I said. There was silence on the other end. I could tell that Al was unable to answer the going well question. "Well, how did the strategic planning conference go and how did you play?" I said to break the silence.

"I played great. Best round of my life. The conference was terrible," Al responded.

"Well, I'm glad something went well. Tell me about your round."

"You can't believe what I shot!" Al related his experience using Swing to Balance. He shot 84 and even three putted four times. "Could have broken 80!" he said with excitement.

"You can't believe" is the statement everyone makes when they have experienced a breakthrough in performance.

"But I started to hook the ball on the last couple holes. What's causing that?" he demanded.

I laughed and said, "It's the golf gods. They won't let you break 80. You aren't ready for that. It's that self-fulfilling prophecy thing. Your muscle memory knows you are a 17 handicap and you're not allowed to be better than that, yet," I added.

"What causes me to hook like that?" he asked.

"It's your old lawn mower swing in combination with Swing to Balance. The muscle memory of your old swing is still there. When you encounter a tough hole, you won't trust the new swing. Was there water on the hole where you started hooking?"

"Yeah. How did you know?" he asked.

"It's like business. When the going gets tough the tough get going," I laughed. "When you encounter a tough hole, your logical self takes control. Your logical mind only knows the old swing, and that is the only thing you trust at that time. It can also be the result of your legs getting tired," I suggested.

"I was getting tired, but I told myself to Swing to Balance before the shot." Al paused for a moment and added, "But you're probably right, I tried to hit it harder because it was over water."

"That's when it happens," I suggested. "When you try to hit it hard rather than swing smooth, the hook or slice will grab you," I laughed.

"The same is true in business. Everyone intends to swing smooth and be partners until business conditions turn tough; then the hit the numbers harder management style returns, snuffing out the teamwork stuff," I suggested.

"That's exactly what happened at the strategic planning conference. The chairman got up and told us to scrap the team stuff. We're going to work smarter this year. Everyone left feeling like dummies. We've spent millions on creating teams and now it's out. I can't believe it," Al added.

"That's very common, Al. Have you ever changed your golf swing in the middle of the round based on a tip from a playing partner?" I asked.

"Yeah. Messed me up big time," Al said.

"Your chairman is causing the organization to oscillate from teams to individual action. I'll bet he also announced a reorganization?" I asked in a joking sort of way.

"How did you know? Sounds like you were there," he said.

"Al, I've been to hundreds of strategic planning retreats and have watched many companies oscillate between harder and smarter. I've watched golfers try tips from the golf magazines and get messed up beyond all comprehension. After they try all the tips, they don't know what swing to swing. One of my friends claims he has 450 categorized golf swings. He tries something new on every hole."

"We'll that's why I called. I want to get together for another lesson, but I also want to talk to you about my job. I'm not sure I can be committed to the new direction. I don't know how I'm going to break the news to my team that we're going back to the old ways."

Al and I agreed to get together for a lesson. I also suggested that we meet at my office concerning his job. Al was vice president of Operations for Galexey Incorporated. I only knew Al from the golf course. I knew of Galexey from having met with the vice president of Sales concerning business development several years ago. I recalled his name was Ron. Ron was a good golfer and the type of person who knows everything about selling.

The president of the Galexey, Rene Simon, is frequently quoted in the paper concerning leadership. She is on the board of directors of the chamber of commerce. According to Ms. Simon, Galexey is aggressively transforming to teams. Her public message is always positive and consistently guarded—"Results are encouraging, but competitive pressures are continuing to affect stock performance."

Al arrived late for our appointment. He seemed down.

"Hi, what's going well?" I asked.

"Why do you always ask me that?" he replied. "Today, nothing is going well. I had to lay off the two people who were doing the team training and cut the rest of the training out of the budget. We cancelled the ropes course events scheduled for the next two months. Everyone was looking forward to that experience," he dejectedly added.

"That's sad. I'm sorry to hear that. I'm sure it wasn't easy to do," I said. Al just looked whipped. "It's like hitting it in the water on the last hole when you are about to break 80 for the first time," I suggested. There was a long pause and I said, "Well, we can wallow in self pity or focus on something that's going well. What do you want to do?"

"Some days it just doesn't feel like anything is going well. You know the feeling?" Al asked.

"Sure do, but if you don't get over it, you'll end up depressed. That's why I asked you what's going well. You're alive and you have a new golf swing under development, so let's focus on that. Okay?" I suggested.

I didn't know Al's business context. Some people love misery at work and are determined to keep it. Al didn't seem to be one of those types, but this was my first encounter with Al focusing on business and I wasn't sure whether he would snap out of the state he was in. The ability to control your state is a very important skill in golf.

"Yeah, that's true, but my work life is *not going well!*"

Al handed me his resume and asked, "Know anyone who needs a good operations manager?"

"When did you do this?" I asked.

"Last weekend. I told my wife I'm serious about not doing this anymore. It's too tough on my people. We keep changing things and after a while nothing is working."

"Just like your old golf problem, right?" I suggested.

"What?"

"You told your wife you were going to resign from the Club. Right?"

"That's exactly right."

"You were going to quit something you really enjoyed because you were frustrated by the process. Right?" I asked. "Maybe there is something similar between golf and your work experience? Your behavior and communication with your wife are exactly the same," I suggested.

"Tell me what you mean?" Al demanded.

"Al, that's your muscle memory in action. It is your reactive self rather than your proactive self. When you are confronted with something that frustrates you, you tend to want to quit or run away rather than deal with the situation objectively or logically. We all have a fight or flight mechanism. Sometimes it is useful. Sometimes it is our biggest enemy," I explained.

Al looked at me with a very strange stare. I could tell I had hit a tender nerve.

I quickly changed the subject by asking, "Tell me about the strategic planning conference in Florida. I'd like to know exactly what happened there. With a deeper understanding of what happened, I may be able to explain your reaction in a different way. Tell me how the session was conducted and what was the outcome?"

"We did the typical SWOT analysis. You know, strengths, weaknesses, opportunities and threats. We've done it that way ever since Rene became president. She brought in a professor from Harper State to facilitate the session. He was good, but he only did what Rene wanted him to do."

"Tell me about the SWOT analysis. What were the dominant themes is each category? I don't know much about your company other than what I've read in the papers."

"Well, our strengths are the same as last year—product quality and our people. We have a great reputation for high quality products, but that leads to high prices. The Sales Department is always arguing for lower prices. That's putting pressure on my group to lower costs. That's why we started the team building thing."

"What were the weaknesses?" I asked.

"Our weaknesses are shipping cycles. We can't meet our delivery promises. The sales people are really frustrated. It's not my fault. If we didn't have all those specials going through the system, we could ship on time. Engineering is bogged down with all the special designs," he added.

"Another weakness is our information technology system. We spent $24 million on a new system in the past two years and most departments are still having problems with it. It doesn't work across the functional boundaries very well. We kept our old system in Operations. We were unwilling to let go and make the complete change based upon the problems they were having in Accounting," Al offered.

"Were there more or less weakness than last year?" I asked.

"Oh, a lot more. It all got blamed on the team training. The team training slowed down decision making. That's why the chairman scrapped it," Al suggested.

"There's always something visible to blame, isn't there?" I suggested.

"What do you mean by that?" Al asked.

"It's like golf. You thought your problem was the new driver. That is something you can see. In business it always appears to be the people because you can see them," I explained.

"You can say that again. My group is being blamed for all the problems. We can't build all the specials fast enough. We can't get the parts in from suppliers. Every special requires a modification in the software and circuit boards. Now they want me to stop the team meetings so we can focus on production. It's a mess."

"What were the opportunities?" I asked, not wanting to hear more justification of the weaknesses.

"We had a tough time identifying any opportunities. The opportunity is to do *more with less*. According to the chairman, we need to work smarter again. Two years ago that meant develop teams. This year it means scrap the team thing. We all feel like a bunch of dummies," Al cynically said.

"Anything else?" I asked.

"Oh yeah. Our biggest competitor has announced a lower priced model in our core business. There's no way we can produce to that cost in our current facility. We would have to build a new plant and that would cost at least $100 million. I guess that's what smarter means," he added.

"Sounds like the golf club business to me. Anything else?" I asked.

"We talked a lot about the impact of the Internet and doing business online, but we have to get the information technology thing figured out first. The IT manager is new and he is optimistic. Wait till he's there a year. He'll find out," Al said.

"Oh, one more. The vice president of Sales says we need to develop what he calls partnerships with customers. He accused me of being the barrier to partnerships. It will never happen. I can't get our suppliers to think like partners. They've all raised prices in the last year."

"What about the threats?" I asked.

"I'm not sure what they came up with. I was so mad at Sales that I left when they listed those. I had three calls from my office that took an hour. By the time I got back the threats were done."

"What seemed to be the main issue?"

"Competition. They're doing things we can't do. We had the teams working on some of that stuff, but now we'll have to put it on the back burner," Al added.

"Also, the government is a threat. If the EPA has its way, we'll get shut down," he suggested. "Don't get me started on the government,"

"No wonder the conference didn't feel right. Let me ask you one more question. Did the group come up with a vision for the future?" I asked.

"Vision! That's a dirty word in our organization. Two years ago the chairman was preaching vision. Two years ago the entire planning conference was about vision and all we came up with was world class. Whoopee do! We can't ship to Chicago let alone the world. What a waste of time," Al protested.

"You're a consultant. You teach golf and leadership. What would you have done if you had been our facilitator?"

"Every consultant has an approach to their business. The SWOT analysis is good. I've used it for years. Today, I use what I call Strategic Visioning rather than strategic planning. It's like Swing to Balance. It's a different approach," I suggested.

"How is it different?" Al asked.

"The short answer is it's based on creating the future rather than problem solving the current situation. It's like Swing to Balance. I helped you begin to create the muscle memory of a perfect golf swing rather than problem solve your existing swing. The Strategic Visioning approach is far more effective as you found out with Swing to Balance."

"It sounds confusing," Al suggested.

"Al, it's the difference between swing the club and hit the ball. It's all about the commands that come out of the planning conference. We could talk all day about what I do, but that is not why you came here today. I have a lunch appointment, so I don't have much time left this morning," I suggested.

"I'm sorry. I was late," Al said.

"Don't be sorry. Let's focus on your personal problem, then we can talk about the company situation. Okay?"

"Well, here's my resume. What do you think? I used one of those resume formats on the computer. Do you think this looks good?" he asked.

"Al, the first question is, are you really committed to finding a new job? Have you resigned or are you just reacting to being frustrated and mad? Remember the golf course? You were frustrated and resigned because you had no solution for your problem. When you found the answer, you decided to stay. Let's be sure you are quitting for the right reason," I suggested. "Your people likely need you to stay."

Al was silent. I continued, "Al, why are you quitting? To resolve your anger or to create a new future? You can hit balls or Swing to Balance. They are different choices."

Al was still silent, not knowing what to say.

"Al, I've watched thousands of people pay golf with a swing that will not produce results. They buy new clubs thinking the club will help, and like you they go deeper into frustration. I've watched companies use a planning process that will not produce results. They buy new technology to fix the problems only to find out that new technology leads to frustration. The golfers either quit the game, like you were going to do, or resign themselves to being handicapped. The companies tell their stockholders to be patient, hoping the new technology will pay off soon. It's all an illusion," I suggested.

"An illusion? What do you mean by that?" Al asked.

"There is nothing wrong with having a golf handicap. We all have one. It enables us to compete on a level playing field and enjoy the game. Unfortunately, in business there is no handicapping system. A company can survive in a handicapped state, but their future is doomed because people like you will get frustrated and leave. If you want to produce results in golf, you must learn to Swing to Balance. If you want to produce results in business you need to learn the skills of leadership. When times get tough, more tough management is an illusion," I suggested. "Most companies today are over managed and under led," I added. "They try to hit the numbers smarter. That is the illusion."

Al thought for a moment and said, "I hate those guys who have a 10 handicap and play to a 5. They don't put in all their scores. I have a 17 and get beat all the time by guys who get more strokes than me. The handicap system is an illusion," he added.

"Al, the handicap system isn't the illusion. Cheating is the illusion. The fact that people cheat doesn't make the system wrong. The same is true in your business. Our democratic system of government isn't wrong even though people often cheat within the system. You need to be accurate in defining the illusion," I added.

"Well I don't like the handicapping system," he protested.

"I don't care for it myself, but until it is changed, I must accept it as the system. I can work to change the system, but I can't make myself miserable by blaming people for cheating. They know what's right and wrong. They choose to live an illusion that cheating will get them what they want. That's a leadership issue," I suggested.

"Al, I have to go. Let's make a list of things to discuss the next time we meet and find a time for your next golf lesson. We need to deal with that hook," I laughed.

The list was rather short. Al was still angry and wanted to talk about his resume. I could tell that the discussion about living an illusion went over his head. His tension was too high to allow the leadership agenda to matter. As we parted, I was sure I would see Al again at the driving range, but I doubted if I would see him again about his job search.

Hi, this is Al. My conversation with Tom shocked me into thinking about things differently. If Tom had not done wonders with my golf swing, I would have been insulted by his statement about my muscle memory in response to conflict. He was right. I do tend to quit easily or at least try to figure it out on my own. I hate asking for help.

The journey you are beginning to read about not only changed my golf game, it changed my business career and my life. I don't want to be dramatic, but we all have lucky learning experiences in our lives. The Swing to Balance lesson on the range that day in October was the beginning of a major shift in thinking for me. From hit the ball to swing the club sounds too simple to be profound, but it is the context shift that I needed.

When I left Tom's office that day, I was confused and felt a little put down. He did not give me the answers that I wanted. He did not confirm that I was justified in wanting to quit and that the handicap system was corrupt. I didn't know it at the time, but we all start a journey toward change by waging war against external circumstance. In my case I was convinced that my company (the chairman, the president, and the Sales manager) were conspiring to get me. I was hooking the ball on the course and at work. I could not keep playing the game of golf or business that way.

I tried Swing to Balance when Tom gave me the video two years ago and it didn't work. I started wondering why I had the answer in my hands two years ago and didn't realize it? Why can't we read Golf Magazine or watch the Golf Channel and do what we read or see? What is this monster called muscle memory? What is the process of translating what you read and know into muscle memory? Do you need the help of a trained professional?

As for Tom on that October day, he was not a golf professional. I knew that his son was a teaching pro. I knew that Tom was a good player, but I did not see him as a qualified instructor. I was reluctant to submit myself to the untrained knowledge of a tipster. I had tried many tips from my playing partners only to be more confused than before. No offense to Gary, but even the pro had me so messed up I wouldn't listen to anyone. I was determined to work it out for myself. No trust is an incredible barrier to change.

As my journey to Swing to Balance unfolds, I will tell you more. Rest assured that what you are about to read is the most amazing thing I have ever learned and it had a significant impact on all the people who work for me. My wife and family are totally different because of the Swing to Balance lesson I was fortunate to receive that October day.

Chapter 3
"Trust Your Swing, Daddy"

Al and I agreed to meet on Thursday evening at the local driving range that has heated tees. It was mid-November and the range at the Club was closed. Al is right, I teach golf as a hobby. We incorporate the golf metaphor into our leadership consulting work, but I do not teach golf professionally.

"Hello." It was Al's wife Susan. "Sorry to hear that. Tell him we can do it next week. Sure, I understand. Tell him to call me when he gets back."

Al had to go out of town to resolve an emergency customer problem and would not be available for the lesson tonight. Susan went on to tell me how excited Al was after the Swing to Balance lesson. She had never seen him so excited about golf.

"Susan, would you like to see Al that excited about his work again?" I asked.

"That will never happen. He's so discouraged about his job. This customer problem is a classic example of the Sales Department promising more than the Operations Department can deliver. I don't think he can handle it much longer," she said in an emphatic tone.

"I know. I see many executives in the same situation. Many of them quit their current job only to find the same thing at their next job," I suggested.

"Why is it that way?" Susan asked.

"It's a long story, but basically most organizations are not programmed to Swing to Balance. It's just like golf; they're programmed to hit the numbers."

"Programmed? Is that what Al is talking about when he talks about muscle memory?" she asked.

"That's right," I said.

"Al told me that what you taught him is so simple, but he never explained what he meant by Swing to Balance."

"It is simple but it is not easy to do. I'd love to explain it to you, but I just don't have time right now."

"I'm sorry," she said.

"Don't be sorry. It's a great thing for everyone to learn. Let's do this. Would you do Al a favor starting next week?" I asked.

Sure, what's that?"

"Do you and the children say goodbye to him when he leaves for work?" I asked.

"Sure.

"Well, starting Monday, just tell him to *Trust his Swing at work*. Instead of saying bye or have a nice day, tell him to *Trust your Swing today*. The children can say, *Trust your Swing, daddy*."

"What will that do?" she asked.

"Initially it will confuse him, but it is the command that will transform how he thinks and acts at work. It will potentially have the same impact as Swing to Balance has had on his golf attitude. I'm sorry, but I don't have time to explain it further right now. Try it and we'll see how it plays out," I suggested. "I promise it will be different for him if he learns what *Trust your Swing* means at work."

"Okay, we'll all do it to him starting Monday morning. Thanks for helping Al. He really appreciates what you've done," she added as she said goodbye.

As I hung up the phone, I chuckled to myself, knowing that Al would wonder what Susan and the kids meant by *Trust your Swing, daddy*. He would quickly figure out that I told them to say that. I was sure he would call me first thing Monday morning, and just like clockwork he called. The following message was on my voice mail.

"Hey, this is Al. Give me a call this morning. It's urgent."

When I called, I got his voice mail and left the following message.

"Hey, this is Tom returning your urgent call. I'm in the office. Swing to Balance."

Within ten minutes Al called. "What this *Trust your Swing, daddy* thing? Did you put them up to that?"

"Of course I did. Who else would do that?" I laughed.

"I don't have a clue what that means here at work. That's a golf swing command."

"I want you to think about that command in two ways today. The verb of the command is to *Trust*. I want you to write down everything you trust today. If the Sales VP calls, I want you to be consciously aware of whether you are trusting him."

"That's easy! There's no way I trust Sales after that trip last week," Al protested.

"Okay, just note how many things you trust and don't trust. Don't judge it. Just realize how much of your working day you spend trusting or not trusting something. You trust the machinery in the plant to be safe, right?" I asked.

"Well yes, if you put it that way, but I don't trust many people outside our group. They're all out to get us," he said in a convincing voice.

"Maybe so," I suggested. "For now, just record when you trust and don't trust. Okay?" I asked. There was silence. "Is that too much to ask?"

"Well, I'm busy and I'm not sure I'll have time to write everything down. I'd be writing all day," he protested. "What does my swing mean?" he asked in a cynical tone.

"In golf the swing is the dynamic process that enables the club to hit the ball," I said.

"Say that again," Al said.

"In golf the club moves because you swing it, right? The swing is dynamic. You swing the club, the club strikes the ball, and your body ends up in Balance. The same is true in your business. Every organization must have a dynamic swing that moves materials to customers with speed and ends up in Balance. Right?" I asked.

There was silence, then Al said, "Yeah, I never thought about it that way. We've done a lot of process redesign recently to make the customer service process go faster. Everything would work if the sales people wouldn't sell specials," he protested.

"Yes, golf would be great if all the fairways were straight, no bunkers, and we didn't have to chip and putt, right?" I suggested.

"Now I am confused," he said.

"Just do this for this week. We can only take one lesson at a time. Record every time you trust and don't trust and we'll look at your list on Thursday evening. Can you do that?" I asked.

"Are you going to charge me a consulting fee for this?" he asked.

"Sure, why not?" I joked. "It will change your life," I laughed.

"There isn't any money in the budget for consulting fees," he began to say.

"Write it down Al. You don't trust me. I'm not going to charge you for anything yet. I'll let you know before I run the meter on you," I laughed. "Remember the golf lesson? It was free," I added.

"Remember our goal this year is to do more with less, and believe me I don't have any money in the budget for consulting fees," Al added.

"Stop it Al. Do you have a piece of paper handy?" I asked. "Then write it down right now, you don't trust me. Can you hear yourself not trusting what I'm telling you?" I added.

"I trust you!" he protested.

"No you don't. You questioned my motives two times. That's no trust. Write it down. You need to realize that your muscle memory is programmed not to trust." There was silence. I could tell that I had hit the tender nerve again.

"Al. Are you there?" I asked.

"I'm here," he said. "I think I get what you are saying about muscle memory. It is deep, isn't it?" he suggested.

"I want you to improve your golf game and your game at work, but you can't do that as long as you don't trust me or the people you work with. No trust leads to frustration and anger and you'll take that anger out on the ball and other people. When you are angry you will hit the ball and hit the sales guy. Does that make sense?" I asked.

"Sometimes I do pretend that the ball is the sales guy. Especially when I hit it in the water. There are some days when I wish they would get lost," he laughed.

"I'm glad you're laughing. Try to record the trust and no trust situations at work today. You now have me on the top of the no trust list. So keep building your list and we'll look at it on Thursday at the range. Okay?" I suggested.

"But I trust you," he protested.

"That's true in some ways. Try to figure out how you trust me and don't trust me. It is both. The same is true with the sales guy. Just write it down.

As I hung up, I chuckled once again. It is amazing how many people are embattled at work trying to hit the numbers at the expense of other people. Sales people must make their quota. Operations must meet their cost objectives. Finance must make the bottom line profit. Some people don't know what number to hit. They're just told that the company doesn't have enough and to be careful not to waste things. Everyone has an excuse as to why they can't hit the numbers. They typically blame other functional people in their own organization. In Al's case, he would hit his number if the sales guy wouldn't sell specials. Or worse yet, they all blame the market or competition or the government for their handicapped condition.

What if they all knew how to Swing to Balance together? I wonder how it would feel. Knowing that some of my clients had integrated the Swing to Balance process into their organizations gave me confidence that I could help Al. It is such a long journey. The muscle memory of the old game is very deeply imbedded. It takes time to transform the golf swing. It takes time to transform the dynamic balance of any organization as well.

Hi this is Al. Well, you can imagine that I was shocked when my two children told me to Trust your Swing, daddy. Then when my wife kissed me goodbye and said, Trust your Swing today, I nearly lost it. What was going on? As I drove to work, I remembered that I had told Susan to call Tom and cancel my lesson. It had to be something Tom had put her up to.

After my talk with Tom, I was conscious all day about trust. It was amazing how nontrusting I found myself at work. It was evident even with my own people. One of my best supervisors complained about a new work procedure and I could feel myself not trusting his motives. I talked to three sales people from major suppliers and didn't trust any of them. They told me that they were giving us their best price on some critical parts and I didn't trust they were telling me the truth.

Asking me to be aware of how and when I trust was a major eye opener. I could not imagine having a day where I could Trust My Swing at work, what ever that meant.

Tom reminded me that I trust the machinery in the plant. It was like trusting that the brakes on my car would work. I then began to think about how I had to trust that other drivers are committed to driving on their side of the road. That made sense, but I had never thought about how much trust we must have within an organization for it to function properly. I then realized that we are strict on the budget because we don't trust people to spend money wisely. That made me mad because I realized how much senior management didn't trust me.

Well, I was hooked. Swing to Balance was beginning to take on more meaning. Stay with me. You will be fascinated by what I learned.

Chapter 4
Capability

Snow was in the forecast for Saturday. Al was anxious to get together for another lesson. The national sales meeting was in January in Scottsdale and he wanted to be ready for the sales guys. We agreed to meet at the local driving range where the heated teeing areas made it tolerable

Al was early. I had already warmed up and was swinging rather well.

"Hi, what's going well?" Al asked as he greeted me.

"My swing," I replied. "That's an interesting question for you to be asking me," I suggested. "Getting comfortable with that question?"

"I tried it at work the other day and my managers were speechless. They didn't know how to answer the question. I told them we want things to go well, don't we? They all agreed but everyone felt intimidated by the question."

"Intimidated? What did they mean by that?"

"They thought I was being cynical and trying to catch them in a lie?" Al said.

"Really? No trust in action," I suggested.

"You know, it's the other shoe syndrome. We all went to a seminar once where we were taught to manage by walking around and when we did that, everyone learned to see us coming," Al said.

"Al, we can talk about business or we can work on your golf swing, but it will be difficult to do both." Al agreed and quickly changed the subject.

"The hook is fierce. Watch," Al said. He took a nice swing at the ball, ended in Balance, and the ball went straight.

"Nothing wrong with that one," I said.

"I can't believe it. Well, wait a few more and it will show up," he said.

It was almost as if Al wanted it to happen. He wanted me to somehow feel sorry for him if it happened.

"Try this," I said. "Let your right elbow pull the lawn mower cord and then Swing to Balance."

Al lurched and snap, the hook happened.

"There it is—see!" he said almost with glee.

"I see. Amazing shot. Some day you'll want to hook the ball out of trouble and you'll need to remember how to do that."

"I'll never want that thing," Al argued.

"Al, all shots are useful. You just need to know how to produce them. You don't need that one off the tee," I suggested.

For the next ten minutes I showed Al why the hook happens even when his swing ends in what he thinks is Balance.

"You can now see that there is a position called fake finish. We think we are in Balance, but we are only half way there. You will see that you are still standing on your right foot. The toe is not straight up. The key is the club plane going back and through the swing," I said.

"So how do I fix it?" Al asked.

"Al, you can't fix it. You must never forget that fixing is the wrong approach. We must create the muscle memory of the correct swing," I said.

I showed Al what we call the Toll Booth position. "The Toll Booth is that narrow slot through which the club must travel on the backswing for the club to be on plane. Imagine you are driving down a tollroad and coming to the tollbooth. You must go slow through that narrow slot, throw money in the basket, then move on. With the lawn mower swing the club misses the Toll Booth every time," I said.

"Here, try it this way. Hold the club with only your right hand. Put the back of your left hand under your right elbow, and turn to the top of the swing." Al tried it and his right elbow quickly disconnected from his left hand due to the lawn mower movement of the right elbow. "That is called a disconnect. If you disconnect going back, you must reconnect coming down, and that is very difficult to do. A disconnected swing will always hook or slice," I said. "If we can create the muscle memory of turning through the Toll Booth you won't hook," I suggested.

Al tried it again and had difficulty staying connected. "Keep the back of the left hand connected to the right elbow. I want you the feel the linkage of the left shoulder to the right elbow."

Al tried it and could feel the connection.

"This is the connection you need with the sales guys. If you disconnect from sales, you'll have a violent hook," I suggested.

"I thought we weren't going to talk about business," he said.

"I'm sorry, but this is a very important leadership point. I thought I would plant the seed so we can recall it later," I said.

"Why is the Toll Booth so important?" Al asked.

"If you swing the club properly, the club will always be perpendicular to the axis of rotation, which is your spine. Notice the club and spine relationship at Set-up. When you get your rear end up and behind you, the angle at Balanced Set-up is 90 degrees. When you turn through the Toll Booth, the club is maintaining that perpendicular relationship to the spine. If the club goes through the Toll Booth, it will travel on the correct club plane during the rest of the backswing."

"Where did you learn this? It is all so basic but it isn't easy to do," Al said.

"Someday I'll tell you where I learned it, but for right now let's continue with your lesson," I suggested. "Set-up, look at the target, turn the club through the Toll Booth—then—Swing to Balance." I watched as Al practiced the move. "Can you feel your body turning the club rather than your hands pulling it back around you body?" I asked. Al nodded. "Great. Do it again." Al took a full swing and ended in balance. "Great Swing!"

Al was back in Balance. All the shots were going a little right, but the contact was solid and the hook was gone.

"What is causing the ball to go right?" he asked.

"The ball is going right because you are turning your head with the body on the down swing. This is a common error even with tour players."

"Here let me show you. Let's do it in animated form first. Slow and easy now. It is important to feel the muscle positions before trying to install them."

I held Al's head as he started to swing down. He could feel his head starting to release as he started down.

"Wow! That's different!" he said.

"That's a great statement," I said.

"What?" he asked.

"That's *different* is a great statement," I suggested. "I teach people to use that phrase in my leadership seminars. After you get comfortable with *what's going well,* I'll teach you to ask your people *what's different* today from yesterday? It's the rate at which you can experience different that keeps you out front in the market. Thought I'd throw that in as long as you are experiencing it now," I suggested.

"Now let's try the swing and this time keep the head from turning until after the ball is gone," I said.

"Is this the keep the head down thing?" he asked.

"It is, but that thought is always misunderstood. Try it. Set-up, look at the target, turn the club through the Toll Booth and Swing to Balance," I encouraged.

This time Al kept his head from turning and he cold topped it.

"That wasn't very good. What did I do?" he asked. "Are you sure that's right?"

I laughed and said, "There you go not trusting me again. It's right. It just takes time to build the muscle memory. You actually pulled back out of your spine angle. Your body was afraid of the position it was in. Take three practice swings, keeping you head in that position, then do it again."

This time it worked. "Wow! Look at that!" Al yelled.

Every one at the range could hear the "Wow!" Al was a little embarrassed. "I didn't mean to be so loud," he said.

"That's okay. It's the emotion of joy," I suggested. "When you do something well, you should blow your horn. The same is true with your people. You should ask them to yell a little every day about what they do well."

For the next twenty minutes we just repeated the two things we worked on so far. Turn the club through the Toll Booth and keep the head from turning until after the ball is gone. That was a difficult move for Al, but it started to feel natural after a few swings.

"What is the leadership equivalent to the Toll Booth and keeping the head from turning?" Al asked.

"What makes you think there are leadership principles associated with them?" I asked.

"Everything else seems to be associated with leadership and this is such an important part of the swing. It has to have some leadership meaning," he suggested.

"You're right. It is a very important concept," I added.

"Well?" Al said and paused waiting for me to tell him.

"Al, the golf swing is round. If the head moves too early on the down swing, the club will not swing through the Toll Booth on the forward side of the swing," I said.

"You didn't tell me there was a Toll Booth on the forward swing." Al said.

I demonstrated for Al the Toll Booth concept on the forward swing. "When the club reaches the Toll Booth on the forward swing, it is going 100 miles an hour. If I make you think about swinging through that Toll Booth, you will never be able to do it properly. If you keep your head steady on the down swing it will just happen," I suggested.

"But I want to know how the swing works," Al protested

"Knowing about the swing and installing muscle memory are two different lessons," I suggested. "If you want to know, I'll tell you, but that will interrupt the practice process," I suggested.

"Tell me," Al said. "I want to know the leadership meaning of Swing to Balance."

"The head is only one part of the body. Every body part must perform both a job and role, and do both properly for the swing to be dynamically balanced. The job of the hands is to grip the club. The role of the hands is to travel on the right path during the swing. The job of the eyes is to see the ball, but the role of the eyes is to keep the head from turning too quickly after the club hits the ball. Every part has a job but it is the proper coordination of the parts, the execution of their roles that produces a Balanced Swing," I explained.

"It sounds like teamwork to me," Al said

That's a good way to think about it but it is important to define what we mean by teamwork in terms of jobs and roles. I've seen many companies implement team initiatives and people lose sight of their job responsibilities. They think everything must now be done with consensus. That's what slows things down. They must understand that they will always have a functional job and an interdependent role. They must do both," I explained.

"We had that confusion when we started the team thing. We thought everyone had to have input and agree on everything. We couldn't reach consensus on a lot of things and everything came to a screeching halt. I wish we had thought about it that way. It would have been so easy to understand," Al said with some cynicism.

"In our leadership seminar we call the ability of every functional part of the organization to perform its role, in the right sequence, *capability*. When an organization has capability it becomes *effortless and effective* in serving customers," I explained. "It is a very complicated thing to teach yet very simple to understand. I call it Swing to Balance."

"Is capability another word for teamwork?" Al asked.

"Yes, in a way, but I don't use the word teamwork to describe it," I added.

"Why not?" Al asked.

"As I just said, teamwork is a great concept, but most people have a picture of a team being deployed in a single location. The word team refers to the configuration of the parts and teamwork is the interaction of the parts. People easily embrace teamwork in their own departments, but it is often difficult to visualize teamwork between departments. It's like your current thinking between your group and sales," I said.

"It is almost impossible for my people to think that we are teammates with Sales," Al said. "They are always blaming us for all their problems," he added.

"That's right, Al. That's why I don't use the word teamwork to describe the interaction between departments. The need in business today is for people who are in different locations and different departments to work together effortlessly and effectively. Some consultants call this collaboration. I call it the capability of the organization to elevate the need for effortless interaction between departments. It is far more effective for senior executives to think that everyone has a job and everyone has a role in serving customers. When they start to think that way, the interaction of people becomes a strategic agenda, not just something nice to do."

"Then what is the role of the head in the golf swing and what is it's equivalent in the organization?" Al asked.

"The job of the head is to think and its role is to act as the pivot point for the golf swing. Someday we'll videotape your swing and put it in the computer. We'll draw a circle around your head and you will see how the club actually swings around the head. The leadership equivalent of the head is senior leaders. Their job is to plan the future of the organization and their role is to inspire the people to want to execute the plan," I explained. "You know this, right?" I asked.

"Sure, but why don't senior leaders do it?" he asked.

"Because they are programmed to hit the numbers not Swing to Balance," I suggested.

"Al we need to go. We are out of balls and there are people waiting. If we mix golf and leadership together, we'll be out here all day," I suggested.

"But this is very important to me right now," he said. "I want to understand it."

"We'll have to find a different place to do that," I suggested. "Let's leave it this way. Golf serves as a good metaphor for leadership, and, both games are overtaught and underlearned," I added as I started to walk toward the pro shop.

"What do you mean by overtaught and underlearned?" he asked.

"There is more money wasted on golf and leadership lessons than any other subjects. Well, maybe we should include selling," I added.

"You can say that again. Those Sales guys are always away at a seminar and nothing seems to change," Al said. "My guys never get to go to those exotic spots for training," he added.

"Al, let's sit down inside and write down what we covered in today's lesson. I want you to have something to refer to when you practice again. You can do these things all winter in your family room or basement if you have them written down. Since Swing to Balance is muscle memory programming, you can work on it all winter without hitting balls," I suggested.

Al and I recorded the key swing thoughts from today's lesson. He began to realize that Swing to Balance was far more complex than he initially thought. Even with the complexity, he was able to write it down in a simple form. Set-up, look at the target, turn the club through the Toll Booth going back, keep the head steady through impact, and Swing to Balance. He made a big note not to let the head turn with the body until after the ball was hit by the club.

Al also noted that every part has a job and a role in the swing. He wrote down that the hands hold the club, the eyes see the ball, the arms swing the club, and the feet and legs hold the body in place. He then made a note that they must all Swing to Balance in a dynamic effortless way for the ball to go straight.

He sat there and seemed to be in a trance. He was staring at the note about dynamic effortlessness. He then added the word capability. He drew a circle around it and put a star beside it. He turned to me and said, "Our organization lacks capability. We all know our jobs but we don't swing together as one unit. Is that what you mean when you say *Trust your Swing, daddy?* We should all know our role in the customer service process and be able to trust each other to do it properly?" he asked.

"That is amazing, Al. It didn't take you long to understand the command," I said.

"Once you experience your body swinging a golf club and know how important every body part is in swinging the club, how can you not see it in your organization? It makes perfect sense," he said. "My only question is how do you get everyone to get it?"

"That's a great question. It isn't easy. It starts with a Strategic Visioning session where the vision is Balanced Finish. Make sense?" I asked.

"No," he said. "We didn't have a vision when we did that retreat. All everyone did was complain about my Department," he added.

"Al, I know and I feel your pain. It's like that day on the range. You thought it was your new driver. The cause of the problem is never what people think it is," I suggested.

"Let's do this about your leadership situation. Control what you can control. Next week sit down with your managers and ask them to identify their jobs and their role in making your own Department effortless and effective. You have done a lot of teambuilding so it might come naturally for them. Use the golf swing metaphor. Tell them how all the parts must work together if the swing will be effortless and effective. See what they say and call me."

"What if they don't know?" he asked.

"Then they don't know. Just like you this morning when you arrived. It isn't wrong to be unaware. I'll teach you how to coach them," I laughed. "Maybe then I can run the meter on you," I added.

As Al and I left the range that morning, it was beginning to snow. I could see and feel Al's excitement and frustration. It is always the same. When you learn a new concept, you want everyone to learn it with you now! It doesn't happen that way. The process of building new muscle memory in your golf swing or in your business takes time.

The key is to be willing to practice the new while enduring the old. I tell my clients they must run the old company while building the new. They must trust that the new way will bring different results. Without trust in the Swing to Balance process, they will give up and accept their handicapped state. The only question is whether you will commit the time to creating the new. The tyranny of the old will always dominate the daily work environment. It is the fire-fighting drill we all know so well.

Hi, this is Al. I'm hooked and feel helpless. After that lesson, I knew that Swing to Balance was correct for my golf game, and I knew that Tom was on to something big called capability. We were always talking about the core competencies in our business. Our Human Resources Department had done a competency assessment for every employee. We were told that competency training would improve company performance. While that is possibly true, it is crazy to think that improving eyesight alone will improve the golf swing. You can strengthen your hand muscles and the golf swing won't improve one bit. You might get a linear improvement from all these things, but the real change must be in the capability to Swing to Balance.

This thought plagued me after I asked my management Team to define their role in our own group. They just looked at me with a blank stare. They knew their jobs but not the role. They were all aware of our job in the company. We make that stuff, Sales sells it, Service services it, Engineering engineers it, and Accounting beats everyone up for not doing it at a profit. What a handicapped organization? We aren't bad at playing the game, but our market share has dropped three percentage points in the last year.

I asked the team, "What have we done different in the past six months?" Once again, they gave me a blank stare. We have escaped the new software conversion for now. We had improved many things to lower costs, but nothing was different. We were doing more with less.

I asked the team to rate the effortlessness of our daily life. On a scale of one to ten with one being very difficult and ten being effortless—we were a four. We were hitting balls and we were pretty good at it. I concluded, silently to myself, that if we were playing golf we would have a 12 handicap. Not bad, but certainly way below our potential. I wondered what our handicap would be if the organization could learn to Swing to Balance.

At least I could now see what the command Trust your Swing meant. What an amazing thought. How simple yet so elusive. Stay tuned. Awareness is the first step in the transformation process. Once you are aware of the potential for doing things different, your tolerance for the old game goes away. At least it did for me.

Chapter 5
Change the Context

I was very busy with my business and didn't see or hear from Al for two months. The sales conference in Scottsdale must have done him in.

"Hello." It was Al. "Al! I thought you died," I said

"You're where?"—"Florida? Must be nice to travel to all the nice places."

"Are you on vacation or is this another planning meeting?" I joked.

I listened as Al told me about the conference he was attending. It was about leadership for the new business environment and sponsored by the American Manufacturing Alliance.

"Is it any good?"—"Boring?"—"Why is it boring?"—"Doesn't teach Swing to Balance?"—"There aren't many people who know that concept."—"Because."—"I know they should but they don't."—"Have you been able to play any golf?" —"Good."—"How's your Swing?"—"Getting better?"—"You did?"—"Good."

Al was there with the CEO of Galexey, Bob Rasmussen, and had a chance to tell him about Swing to Balance over dinner the night before. Bob was interested in knowing more about the concept because his new son-in-law had mentioned balance in reference to golf two weeks before.

"Bob wants to meet you," Al said.

"Why?" I asked.

"He's ready to fire the Sales guy and wants to know more about what you mean by the capability of the organization."

"Al, you are amazing," I said.

"We are getting killed in the market because of price. Nothing we do at the manufacturing level seems to matter. We have our costs down. We have teams in place. We're lean and mean. We have focused factories and high commitment work systems and we're still losing market share. It's a Sales problem," Al asserted.

"That may be true, but it's likely a leadership problem. Are you sure the CEO is open to that possibility?" I asked.

"I think I have his attention. I beat him on the golf course yesterday for the first time. He doesn't like it that his son-in-law knows more about golf than he does. When I told him he wasn't Swinging to Balance, he was curious about what I knew about balance."

"Sounds like he feels vulnerable when someone knows more than he does," I suggested.

"That's for sure! He's tough to convince," Al said.

"So, what makes you think that I can teach him anything?" I asked.

"Well, he's in trouble with the board. I can't talk right now, but he's really interested in meeting you," Al said.

When Al returned from Florida, he called and we found a convenient time for me to meet Bob. Our meeting started with the normal bravado about the business environment and how it was difficult to make a buck on anything. It's like golf. There is always a reason why you aren't playing well.

Bob was a nice guy. After the initial banter, he started by saying, "Al told me a lot about you. He said you changed his life."

"That's a stretch, but a new golf swing sometimes feels like a life-changing experience," I suggested.

"Tell me about your background and about this Swing to Balance concept you've developed," he said.

I told him about my background and quickly moved on. "Swing to Balance is not something I made up. I learned it the hard way. I was a driving range junkie. I practiced a lot. Hit thousands of balls. I actually enjoyed hitting balls more than playing. It was my way of relaxing in the evening."

"My son Bill started to play golf at the age of five and we've had a great relationship based on golf for years. Bill was a great player in high school but suffered a sever injury that prevented him from playing in college."

"I was like most dads who had a son coming up in golf. I tried to teach him everything I knew about the game, and it worked until he began playing competitive golf. He started to play junior tournaments when he was eight. When he played well everything was great. When he played bad, it was my fault."

"We would go to the range and work on his swing. You don't need to know the agony. When you are emotionally involved in the process, it is very difficult to be a coach. I'm sure it's like your Sales guy. When business isn't working, you have to have someone to blame," I suggested.

I tried to make some reference to Bob's agenda to see his reaction. When I mentioned the Sales guy, I could see immediate agreement in Bob's body language.

"It's a long story, but I would go to the range, find a grove where I was hitting balls well, and come home and try to show Bill. Problem was, what worked for me didn't work for Bill."

"This created more and more tension in our golf relationship. I would practice well all week and play bad on Saturday. I just couldn't get it to work on the course."

"I have that problem all the time," Bob related.

"We all have that problem and we don't know what to do about it. We think the answer is more practice and we hit another 1000 balls trying to get better."

"What was the answer?" Al asked.

"After Bill's injury, he went to a golf academy to learn about being a Club professional. His playing career appeared to be over. I'll never forget Bill coming home for the holiday and telling me, "I know what's wrong with your golf game dad." That was a real role reversal. I wasn't open to advice on my game. It had always been me giving him advice about his game. You know how dads are?" I suggested.

"Yea, my son-in-law told me something about my game a month ago. It didn't settle well," Bob agreed.

"What did Bill tell you?" Al asked.

"He told me my clubs were wrong and that I did not Swing to Balance," I continued.

"You're clubs were wrong? What did he mean?" Al asked.

"My clubs were to flat. They were not fit to my swing. Worse yet, we eventually found out that my clubs varied from three degrees to flat to three degrees to upright. The only club that was right was my 8-iron. That was the one I practiced with all the time. The rest of the set were way off."

"I had no idea what he was talking about. I defended my clubs. I had used them for ten years. They were Tour Blades! I emphatically told him."

"At that time, I was a solid 8 handicap player. On my best days I could shoot in the 70s, but my normal score was 82. It got to be a joke. My wife would tell me to just post 82 and not go play and spare myself the agony. I would come home and agonize about my game. I would go practice more and nothing got better. I was great on the driving range as long as I was hitting my 8-iron or my driver."

"Bill showed me what he meant by Swing to Balance. I had no idea what he was talking about. When he showed me, I immediately said I had tried that and if I would swing that way, I would either pull the ball left or block it right every time. He said that was because my clubs had the wrong lie angle."

"Gentlemen, to make a long story short, it was very difficult for me to accept that my son knew more than I did about golf. You know, the ego thing. Well that was the beginning of Swing to Balance," I said.

"What happened from there?" Al asked.

"I let go and allowed Bill to teach me. It wasn't easy, but within a year I was Swinging to Balance and able to reduce my handicap to 4. As you said Al, my life was changed."

"The important point for today is to know that Swing to Balance isn't some trick or the latest golf tip. The swing of every professional ends in Balance. It has to or it won't work."

"I started to think about the Swing to Balance concept as it relates to business. I was telling this story to one of my best clients and he said, "Like win-win?" and I said, yeah, Balanced!"

"That was twelve years ago. Since then we have developed the Swing to Balance concept into a leadership model that helps people in any kind of company let go of the old game and learn how to do it different."

"What do you mean by that?" Bob asked.

"Think about what I was doing. I was on the practice range for ten years with the wrong clubs, practicing in a way I could never master. I see executives working the old game, planning the old way, trying to make their companies meet the challenges of the new business environment, using the wrong tools," I said.

"We have all new technology," Bob replied.

"I know you do. Al told me about the conversion, but is it working?" I asked.

"Yes and no," Bob said.

By now Bob was ready to tell me about his situation. He had heard enough about my saga on the driving range. He was ready to talk.

"I'm not sure that our situation is similar to your driving range adventure, but we are not meeting the expectations of our board of directors. We have missed the budget for the second straight year. The Sales vice president just doesn't have a clue."

Bob related what I already knew from discussions with Al. Orders for specials were taxing the system. The Sales people were unable to sell standard products, and the manufacturing system was being blamed.

"We thought it was our manufacturing system for a long time, but Al has convinced me that we have done everything possible in the plant. We have teams. We have cooperation between labor and management. It's a sales problem. We just aren't getting our share of the market," Bob confirmed with confidence.

"What are you doing to correct the sales problem?" I asked.

"Frankly, I'm not sure what to do. I'm ready to fire the VP of Sales and get someone in here who can make it happen."

"Make what happen?" I asked.

There was silence. Bob didn't know how to respond. I could tell he thought I was being confrontational.

"Well, Al suggested that you might know and that Swing to Balance had something to do with it. Based upon what I've heard so far, it doesn't sound like you have the answer either," Bob confidently stated.

I could feel the defensiveness in Bob's voice.

"Tell me what you do for companies in these types of situations?" he asked.

"Bob, I appreciate the seriousness of the situation. You are in a crowded boat right now. Very few people have the answers. Almost every company has made widespread systems changes, converted to teams, empowered the people, cut costs, and hired new sales people. The game is going faster, but companies are still falling behind. To use the golf metaphor, you have all the new clubs and an old swing. The key is to change the context about how you think about what you are doing from hitting balls to swing the club," I said.

Before Bob or Al could speak, I continued, "Bob, I have very limited knowledge of your situation. All I know is what Al and you have told me, but it is symptomatic of what I see everywhere. Many executives are trying to address a leadership situation with management skills. Every CEO I know has tried to hit the numbers with more determination and it doesn't work. They first have to change the way they think about the game. That's called changing the context of the situation. That's a leadership skill," I suggested.

By now I was making Bob very uncomfortable. I had implied that he lacked leadership skills. I could see Al squirm in his seat. This wasn't what he had hoped to have happen.

"Let me give you an example of what I mean by changing the context that constrains an organization. If you see the world as flat, you will naturally build flat world boats. If you see the world as round, you would be able to build round world boats. The problem is you can't build round world boats in a flat world factory. In your case, it isn't that you can't build specials. The context of your factory is mass production and a mass production business model is not friendly to customized orders. The context of mass production is the problem," I explained.

I could tell that Bob was a quick study. He grasp the flat world analogy and asked, "What is the new context for the factory?"

"It's called Mass Customization," I said. "It requires a new business model and new leadership skills at all levels of the organization."

Bob said, "I'm open. It could be me. I have a son-in-law trying to tell me about my golf game and I'll bet he's right. Your son was right. It could be my old game. How would I find out?" he asked.

I could see the shocked look on Al's face. He had just witnessed a breakthrough in thinking.

"Frankly, a change in context would be good for every executive in this company," Bob added. "We have run this company hitting the numbers for years. That is all we know. Maybe we all need to think about it different. How would we do that?" he asked.

Bob's assistant interrupted our meeting. The chairman was on the phone with an urgent need. Bob had to take the call and he was already late for a lunch appointment. We decided to pick up the conversation from here at a later time.

This is Al. I almost lost it that morning. I had invited Tom to meet with Bob to explain the Swing to Balance process. Little did I think that I would be on the brink of getting fired. If Bob had not responded to the question, "Make what happen?" the way he did, it might have been all over for me.

I had a good relationship with Bob but there was always a separation. Bob never let himself be vulnerable like that.

There was something about the way Tom approached the situation, however that made it work. It wasn't about what Tom knows versus what Bob knows. That round world --flat world analogy made sense to Bob. It was as simple as hitting balls versus swinging the club. Something clicked for Bob. I'm not sure what his son-in-law said, but the story about Tom's son must have been similar.

Many meetings start and end and very few reach closure. Bob's approach is to always say we have a lot on our plate right now and we need to think about what to do next. Bob, Tom and I agreed to meet again within ten days to talk more about golf, but somehow I knew Bob was serious about changing how we were leading the organization. Stay tuned.

Chapter 6
"What Is It?"

Al and I left the meeting with Bob in silence. I could tell that Al was both concerned and excited about what had happened.

"Got time for lunch?" I asked.

Al looked at his watch and said, "Fine. Let's go somewhere we can talk."

We decided on Max & Erma's and agreed to meet there in twenty minutes.

As we sat down in the restaurant Al asked, "How do you think the meeting went?"

"I thought Bob was open and actually very receptive to a new way of seeing the business. What did you think?" I asked.

"I almost lost it when you asked him, make what happen? I've seen him take people's heads off for questioning his thinking."

"Al, that is the most difficult thing about leadership consulting. Bob, in his manager Bob job, will be very difficult to work for. He has an intimidating style and people will learn not to question his thinking. That keeps the organization in control and in compliance with his wishes."

"You can say that again. You should see Bob and Ron argue about sales."

"Who's Ron?" I asked.

"Ron Walters is the VP of Sales who's on his way out if he doesn't make it happen soon."

"Does Ron play golf?" I asked.

"Yeah, he's a good player, probably a 4 handicap. Why? Do you think you can teach him Swing to Balance?" Al asked.

"No. I met Ron three years ago. He was looking for some sales training that would fix the sales problem at Galexey," I said.

"That's right," Al said. "They did some sales training about three years ago, but it didn't work. Did you do the training?" Al asked.

"No. I told Ron at that time that the sales force didn't need to be fixed. I used the golf analogy that you can't fix a golf swing into existence that you've never had," I said.

"What happened?" Al asked.

"He wanted to argue not understand," I suggested.

"That's Ron," Al said. "He never listens to other people's point of view."

"He's going to need to learn new ways soon," I said.

"Why do you say that?"

"Because I think Bob understood the change in context thing. You know, the shift from hitting balls to swinging the club. That part of our conversation made sense to Bob. I think he related it to the sales situation. Other than the sales problem, do Bob and Ron get along?" I asked.

"Ron thinks he knows it all when it comes to golf. He's always trying to give Bob tips on his game. Ron is always making big bets with Bob and he generally wins. Bob is always upset about his golf relationship with Ron," Al related.

"So there's more than a sales performance problem between them?" I suggested.

"You bet. I also heard that Ron interviewed Bob's son-in-law for a sales job last week. Don't know how it went."

"Let's go back to the meeting. Tell me what you think Bob will do as a result of our discussion. He seemed very interested in going to a next step. How does he generally end a meeting with his senior staff?" I asked.

"He always tells everyone to fix the problem and get back to him. He's very good at the details. That's why he's been successful as the CEO. The chairman is that way too. His favorite phrase is make something happen. That's why I almost died when you asked him, "Make what happen?" Al said.

"When you leave a meeting and he's issued the command to fix it or make it happen, do you know what *it* is? In other words, are you able to translate that command into action?" I asked.

"I'm not sure what you mean?" Al paused and said, "We always know what the problems are and when we need to have something done. Is that what you mean?"

"Al, remember the Swing to Balance lesson? I took control of your command center. I put a different command in your brain by telling you to Swing to Balance. Your body was able to execute that command because we had practiced Balanced Finish. It was foreign to the muscle memory of your old swing, but the way I commanded you to execute it was dynamic rather than static. Remember when I yelled at you to Swing to Balance? You just did it."

Al looked at me in a curious way and said, "How can I forget. But what are you trying to say?"

"Changing the way your company operates will not happen because you get a new VP of Sales that can make it happen if no one knows what *it* is. If Ron doesn't know what *it* is, he can't command the sales people to do anything other than hit the numbers. Leadership is all about knowing how to change the command center within the organization," I suggested.

"What should I do with my people? Tell them to Swing to Balance?" Al asked in a rather cynical way.

"That would work if they understood what Swing to Balance means. The word swing is dynamic and balance can be visualized, at least from a golf perspective. If they knew what Swing to Balance means in business terms, it would be an effective command."

"Say that again," Al pleaded. "You lost me on that one."

"Al, it is impossible for people to translate vague commands into specific action. If you ask your son to take out the trash, he will take out the trash, not put the cat out. If you ask a child to be nice, he may just sit quietly on a chair for fear of misbehaving. He may not have any idea what be nice means and just be quiet in fear of making a mistake. Anyone ever tell you to drive safe?

"Sure."

"What safe means to one person is very different to another. The key is to be clear about what you want people to do when you are leading an organization."

"Clear about what?" Al asked. "Give me an example?"

"Watch this. It says right here on the menu that the purpose of Max & Erma's is to *help us enjoy our total dining experience so we can't wait to come back.* If they have imbedded the meaning of that purpose statement in the muscle memory of their employees, the waitress will not only know the statement, she will be able to orchestrate our experience so we will be anxious to come back. Want to find out if it's in her muscle memory?"

Al was a little embarrassed as I asked the waitress the purpose of her job. When she smiled and told us exactly what was on the menu, Al was surprised

"That's amazing," Al said. "How did you know she would know that?"

"The leadership process at Max & Erma's is based on having a job and a role. The leaders of Max & Erma's have worked hard at implementing the process." I said.

After we placed our order, I asked, "Al, what is the vision in your strategic plan from last year's planning session?"

"To be world class," Al said sarcastically.

"Have you and your people begun to create toward that vision?" I asked.

"Are you kidding! We can't figure out how to ship to Chicago, remember?" he said.

"See what I mean. World class is a vague vision that even you can't translate into action. When people are given a command to make it happen over and over again and they are afraid to ask what *it* is, they get cynical, complacent, and apathetic," I suggested. "It is even worse when the senior leader uses the command of fix it. Fix it implies that something is broken and there is someone to blame for breaking it."

"What do you think Bob means by make it happen?" Al asked.

"He probably has a long list of *its*. He probably is implying financial success. Most CEO's are very aware of what *it* is in terms of revenue, costs, profits, market share, stock price, shareholder value—all the numbers stuff, you know hit the ball. That's the context of the Mass Production business model," I suggested.

"We go over the numbers all the time. We all know the numbers," Al said.

"Then there is no mystery about what *it* is that he wants Ron to make happen.

It is probably top line revenue, right?" Al nodded agreement but shrugged his shoulders. "So Bob is commanding Ron to hit the ball in golf terms. Would you agree?" I asked.

"This is going nowhere. Let's switch subjects," he suggested. "I want to know how you went from an 8 handicap to a 2 after your son showed you that your clubs were wrong? You've told me that I don't need new clubs. I'm confused. Do I need new clubs or not?"

"Good question. There are many ways to lower your handicap. The most effective way is to learn to putt," I laughed. "But improvement beyond the 8 handicap level is very difficult. At that point you must improve your swing, not your ability to hit the ball. You know what I mean by that, right?"

"Right," Al said. "Swing to Balance not hit the ball. Got it."

"There are two ways to change the golf swing to improve your game. The first is to manipulate your swing to fit the club. The second is to create a Balanced Swing and then fit the club into the swing," I suggested. "It sounds strange so let me explain," I added.

"Think of all the older players like Palmer, Casper, Chi Chi, Trevino—who all have goofy swings. They grew up with a set of clubs. They had to figure out how to manipulate their bodies to make the club work properly. In other words, the club was the constant and their swing was the variable. They had to figure out how to modify their swing to make the club work. Does that make sense?" I asked.

"So far," Al said.

"In the late 70s and early 80s it became possible to customize the club to fit the swing. That's when what is referred to as the modern golf swing was invented. With a computer they simulated the perfect swing. It is now possible for any person to create a Balanced Swing, then have a set of clubs customized to fit into their swing. It is 180 degrees opposite of how the early players did it," I said. "The Swing is now the constant and the clubs are the variable."

"So when should I get new clubs?" Al asked. "It seems like the chicken or the egg."

"This is the difficult part of teaching Swing to Balance. The clubs can't be customized properly until the student begins to Swing to Balance. Initially, you must learn with your existing clubs even though they may be wrong. That's why I encourage you to work on your swing without hitting balls."

"I get it. Create the swing, and then fit the club to the swing. Is that right?" Al asked. "Hey that's neat! I never thought of it that way," he said with some excitement. "But what if the ball keeps hooking and I'm Swinging to Balance?" he asked.

"That tells me your clubs are probably too upright or the shafts are too flexible. There could be many things that need to be adjusted in your clubs, some of which might not be possible. Then it would be time for you to get a customized set of clubs," I suggested.

"Maybe that is what *it* is?" Al laughed. "Maybe Bob is a club fitter and means we ought to get new clubs to fit the factory."

"He may mean that, but it is likely just the opposite," I suggested. "Today you tell the customer they must accept what the factory wants to make. You are telling the customer to fit their needs to the factory. Make sense?" Al nodded yes with some hesitancy. "When Ron sells a special, the customer is telling you to fit the factory to their needs."

"You are exactly right," Al protested. "And we can't do that," he asserted.

"Think about what you just said. You can do it, but it is opposite of your hit the numbers game. Right?" I suggested. "With new technology it is now possible to customize the factory to fit the customer rather than force the customer to fit the factory."

"Say that again. It sounds like double talk," Al said.

"Let's go back to golf. It's easier to understand. Once my son helped me make the change in context from hit the ball to Swing to Balance, I was able to understand why my clubs didn't work. My 8 iron was perfectly fit to a balanced swing. The rest of my clubs were way off. Once the balanced swing started to feel natural for me, I bought the customized clubs and my handicap went from 8 to 2."

"How long did it take?" Al asked.

"About a year."

"A year! To go from an 8 to a 2. That's amazing," Al said.

"It took about six months to get to a 4 handicap. It took that long for me to trust the Swing to Balance process on the course. I had to change twenty years of old muscle memory. That was not easy to do," I suggested.

"So new clubs changed your swing?" Al asked.

"No. I learned to Swing to Balance using my old clubs. Thinking Swing to Balance versus hit the ball changed my swing. We adjusted the lie angles of my old clubs to match my 8 iron and then I practiced just one thing, Swing to Balance."

"Did it work with the old clubs?" Al asked.

"It was a struggle at first. I could get it to work on the driving range but I couldn't make it work on the course. On the course I was still thinking hit the ball. That was my old muscle memory on the course. It's like your situation with the water hole. What do you trust? Right?" I laughed.

"Stop it!" Al yelled. "Once I started to hook the ball, I tried something different on every hole. I didn't trust Swing to Balance any more."

"Al, we've all done that in search of the magic swing that will survive the round. That's golf for almost every amateur. It isn't until you know your swing that it starts to work. The swing needs to become the constant, not the club."

"When did you buy new clubs?" Al asked.

"Once my swing started to repeat itself. When I was able to Swing to Balance at a constant speed of 105 miles per hour with the driver, I bought clubs to fit that swing."

"How did you do that?" Al asked.

"Al, Bill helped me. Club fitting is a very sophisticated process. It is both an art and a science. It requires the dynamic fitting process that Bill learned about at Golf School."

"Al, I have to go. I'll explain it to you next time we are at the course. The pros at the Club have a fitting system. I'll show it to you."

"Is it that goofy looking cart with all the clubs in it that they take out on the range?" he asked.

"Yes. Gary probably suggested that you get fitted clubs, right?" I asked.

"He did, but they were way too expensive. My wife would've killed me."

"Let's leave it this way. Fitted clubs are like tailored clothes. They will change the emotional memory of your game."

This is Al. There are times in your life that you feel smart and times you feel stupid. After that lunch, I really felt dumb. How could I have played golf all that time without knowing what Tom told me? Then I began to realize that it had happened to him as well. He had played and practiced for twenty years without knowing about fitted clubs and Swing to Balance. Maybe ignorance is bliss?

I was upset with myself for days. I started to ask myself about it. What is it that I need to know that would change not only my golf game but more important my work. The comment about fitting the factory to the customer really twisted my mind. How could that be possible? We always forced the customer to buy what we wanted to make. We were always tinkering with the factory to make our products cheaper and eliminate waste, but we never considered the impact of tinkering on the customer. The constant was our process. We had it down to a science, but we were losing market share. The customers weren't cooperating any more. Customers wanted specials we couldn't make. Maybe the more accurate answer was we could make them, but we wouldn't change our process to fit the factory to the customer.

I struggled with the context of it. Were we the swing or the club? I was confused and wanted to forget it and move on, but I couldn't get it out of my mind. Maybe that is what Tom meant by emotional memory. I couldn't feel the way I wanted to feel. My confidence going to work was shot. If one of my managers would ask me "What it is that we need to make happen," I don't know what I would have said. Probably do what Bob does; just tell them to figure it out. Stay tuned, it gets worse.

Chapter 7
The Business Model

Three days after my meeting with Bob and my lunch with Al, I received an email from Ron. It was rather cryptic saying, "Galaxey Incorporated will be taking bids on a new sales training program and your company has been identified as a possible vendor. The specifications are attached. Please review the requirements and submit your proposal by the time lines listed."

I consult with many clients on business development processes that lead to some form of sales training for their sales staff. In today's business environment how a company sells is actually more important than what it sells. The build a better mouse trap days are over. Today, companies must clear the briars from the path to their door. Customers won't beat a path through the briars any longer. There are companies that are easy to do business with. Partnering has replaced vending as the context for many business relationships.

I looked at the specifications for the requested training. I could immediately see why Ron was having trouble making it happen. I won't bore you with the details, but Ron wanted to fix the sales people once again, and from the time lines in the specifications, he was determined to do it fast.

I recalled Al's comments about Ron. "He's a 4 handicap golfer who continually tries to tell Bob how to play golf." His big bets confirm he's a competitive guy with a strong ego. The specifications for the sales training include a heavy dose of time and territory management and the ability to sell at the executive levels in client organizations. The intensity of Ron's style was very obvious from the email.

I've played golf with many guys like Ron. They are good players. They crush weaker players. They will press the bet with better players hoping that more determination on their part will add pressure to the opponent causing them to crumble. To a Ron, the game of golf is about effort and pressure. They create a constant atmosphere of conflict with their playing partners.

I was very busy on two important projects with other clients and ignored Ron's email for two days. Knowing that Bob probably had told Ron to include me on the bidders list, I felt obligated to respond in some way. My email response said, "I appreciate the opportunity to offer consulting support for the business development initiative at Galaxey Incorporated. To better understand the challenge confronting the sales professionals, I would like an opportunity to understand the dynamics of the existing sales process." I went on to ask if it would be possible to meet with Ron to talk about what it was that he would like to have happen differently once the training was complete.

As I expected, there was no response to my email.

The next week my phone range. It was Al. "What's going well?" I asked.

"Nothing! I tried to get you in the door with Ron and you didn't submit a proposal for the sales training. Do you want to do business with our company or not?" he asked in a cynical tone.

"Yes, I want to help your company, but not as a vendor," I suggested.

"What does that mean?" he asked.

"Ron's request for sales training is a typical vendor approach to acquiring things. I asked if I could come in and understand the situation and what it is that he wants to do different. I know that he did sales training three years ago and it didn't work. So I thought it would be important this time to be sure it works," I explained. "He didn't respond to my email so I didn't send a quote because I don't know what to tell him other than Swing to Balance," I said.

"If you don't send an initial quote, you won't make the bake-off," Al suggested.

"That's okay," I said. "I've been in many bake-offs before and seldom get the business from that process. Vendors in a bake-off situation promise the world then withhold innovation thinking it is just a matter of price. As you know, I haven't started running the meter on you yet, and you have already received considerable coaching."

"That's true, but how are you going to get in with Ron if you don't send a proposal? They are going to pick from the top three proposals," Al encouraged.

"That's a good approach if they know what they want, but based on the specifications, I'm confident they are confused."

"Confused?" Al asked.

"The specifications for the sales training are vague. He's once again trying to fix the sales problem to hit the numbers. The Context is hit the ball. Does that make sense?" I asked.

"But, I thought you could change his Context. That's why I told him to send you a bid package," he added.

"I could change his Context if he would take time to tell me what he wants the sales people to do different as a result of the training. I asked Ron if I could meet with him and I received no response. I can't change his Context by bidding," I suggested.

"That's the way he runs his department. They won't return my emails either," Al said.

"That's a clue about his ability to change," I said.

"Bob really wanted your input on the sales problem. He told Ron to put you on the bidders list so you could get involved," Al added.

"I appreciate Bob's intentions but my services are un-vend-able. Al, you know me well enough by now that I can tell you the truth about the situation. There are sales people who will sell you golf clubs that have no chance of improving your game. There are financial planners that will develop a financial plan for you to sell their mutual funds. There are all kinds of sales training programs. Based upon what Bob told me about the sales situation at Galexey, Ron cannot solve the problem with more sales training designed to make the existing sales people work harder or with more effort. Remember you had to Swing to Balance to change your golf game. You could not hit the ball harder and improve," I explained.

"Are you sure you know what Ron should do different?" Al asked. "He thinks he knows what he needs," he added.

"Al, I don't know for sure because I've not talked with Ron about the situation. But, I've heard enough from you and Bob to know that the sales people need to fit the factory to the customer rather than force the customer to fit the factory. I did a little research on your biggest competitor, and based upon what I see on their web site, they are Swinging to Balance, not hitting balls."

"You need to convince Ron," Al protested.

"I can't convince Ron if I can't meet with Ron," I suggested. "So I guess that's your role," I laughed.

"My role? I'm not going to argue with him ever again," Al asserted.

"Then it's not going to change. I have plenty of work with clients where it is not a contest of wills. I'd be glad to help him make it happen if we could talk about what it is he wants. Golf is a game without conflict Al."

There was silence on the phone. I knew that my emotional bank account with Al was empty. Executives desperately want to fix the factory to make the numbers. They go to the driving range determined to find the solution to their problems. They manipulate their swings over and over again trying to find the right combination of hip turn and weight shift. Ron is going to the sales training range one more time determined to find the solution to the sales problem. It won't work.

Al broke the silence by saying, "Well, maybe it's time to run the meter on us. Bob asked me to call you and find out why you didn't bid. I can't tell him you didn't want to and I don't know how to tell him why you didn't. What should I tell him?"

"Al, I feel your pain. It's like that October day on the range. You were trying one more time to figure it out before you declared it over between you and golf. I'm willing to help, but you need to know that I will not try to win a bake-off with other vendors to do it. Let's do this. Tell Bob that I will be glad to talk with him again about the sales situation. This time I want Ron involved in the conversation. Ron may have a sales training problem, but he likely has a leadership problem. If he doesn't address the leadership issue, the situation will be terminal," I suggested.

"How will you know?" Al asked.

"When we find out what *it* is he wants his sales people to do different." I replied. "Is it hit the numbers harder or Swing to Balance?"

"What does Swing to Balance mean in sales?" Al asked.

"To tell you that, I'll have to run the meter on you. It's a secret," I laughed.

We decided when it might be possible to meet with Ron. The sooner the better and the meeting was set for 9:00 a.m. the next morning.

"Hi, I'm Ron Walters. You must be the Swing to Balance man," Ron said in a rather sarcastic tone. "Haven't I met you somewhere before?" he asked.

"Yes, several years ago at a golf outing, I think. Hi Bob. It's good to see you again. Thanks for the opportunity to help Galexey with the challenges of change," I said.

Bob started the meeting by telling Ron about me, and how I had dramatically changed Al's golf swing.

Ron interrupted saying, "Al had only one way to go and that was up. So I'm not surprised you helped him."

I could see Al bristle but he kept his cool. Bob continued to set the agenda by telling Al and Ron that he had called several of my references and that I had successfully helped other companies with tough sales problems. Everything about Bob's introduction was about my ability to solve the sales problems of Galexey. There wasn't any sense that they might have a leadership problem.

Bob made it clear that I was now on the clock and that Ron would listen to what I had to say. I could see the resistance in Ron.

Ron broke in by saying, "Well tell us what we should do, I'm all ears."

I responded by saying, "Ron, both you and Al know what to do. Customers want specials and Manufacturing can't or won't produce them. Right?"

"That's right. I've been telling Al that for two years now," he said.

"Specials upset the standard flow of product for Manufacturing and cause problems for Engineering. Right Al?" I added.

"The order entry system for a special is impossible," Al replied.

"I'm guessing, but I suspect your sales people are frustrated by losing business and you believe they can gain new business if they will call on new accounts, right? At least that's what your request for proposal asked for. Am I right?" I asked.

"That's right. I want the sales training to teach our sales people to call on new accounts and call higher in existing accounts. They've gotten lazy and won't generate new business," Ron added.

"Then you want your sales people to look harder to find customers that will fit your factory? Is that what I'm hearing you say you want?" I asked.

"You got it," Ron said. "What's the solution?" he asked sarcastically again.

"Your situation is very similar to hundreds of other companies. The bottom line is that the business model you are trying to execute is burned out. It no longer works," I suggested.

"The business model?" Bob asked.

"Yes, the business model. The Mass Production business model looks at the market from the factory and forces the customer to buy what the factory can conveniently make. It is based on the economies of scale. In this model the sales people are told to find customers and convince then that what the factory makes is what they want. Well, it has all changed. With new technology the customer is now the king. They don't need to settle for what is convenient for you to make. They can get it customized the way they want it and they won't settle for anything less. You call their needs specials. To the customer, the need is customization. Does that make sense?" I asked.

Ron jumped in, "I've been trying to tell you guys this for two years."

"Yes, Ron you have, but you've made it a contest of conflict between Sales, Manufacturing, and Engineering," I said.

Defensively Ron interrupted, "How do you know that?"

"For right now, let's just say I know that from my discussions with Al and Bob over the past six months. The important point to make is that the Mass Production business model is causing the problem. It is not a personal issue. You all want the same thing—to play the game different—but you just don't know how to change it. More important, I suspect that some of your customers—the ones that are still loyal to you—are hoping you'll change the game real soon."

"You can say that again," Ron added. "We're about to lose our biggest account. They have been through thick and thin with us and they told me yesterday that they need a special design or they will have to go to the competition."

"Ron, that is what you need to teach your sales people," I suggested.

"Teach them what?" he asked.

"They don't need to know how to find new accounts who won't want specials. Every account will want customization. They need to learn to sell within a new business model and you need to lead them to that awareness," I suggested.

Ron was silent so I said, "In summary gentlemen, the business model has changed and you have a leadership problem not a sales problem. Does that make sense?" I asked.

"How would we train the sales people to do this?" Ron asked. I could tell he was feeling vulnerable in front of Bob.

"You have to start by never calling the customers request specials ever again."

"What would we call them?" Al asked.

"They are customized options. The new business model is called Mass Customization. Ron, you need to teach your sales people how to sell customized options. Al, you need to teach your teams to embrace customization. Bob you need to tell Accounting to figure out how to cost account for customization and help Engineering develop the cafeteria of options within the design of the products. I suspect all of this is being done in some way today by all the groups. So all you need to do is eliminate the conflict that exists between all the departments about this issue. Changing the context from hit the ball to Swing to Balance starts by thinking different. Golf is not a game of conflict."

Once again there was silence. Then something amazing happened. Bob said, "Let's make it happen."

"We already are," said Al. "I just didn't see it that way. This is easy."

Al was correct when he said *it* was already being done. It is true that his factory was already able to customize products but Mass Customization is more than a manufacturing strategy. It is an entirely new business model that affects the entire business. So I said, "Bob, let's make sure we clearly define what *it* is. I'm sure everyone can make *it* happen, but you need to lead this into place not manage it into place. It will require a major change in all three levels of learning within the organization and you cannot underestimate the resistance of the imbedded muscle memory of the old business model. It will be a formidable foe," I suggested.

Al interrupted by asking, "Three levels of learning? What do you mean?"

"Al, it's like golf. You know about Swing to Balance, right?"

"Yeah," he agreed.

"But, training the muscles to know the new swing is a long arduous process, right?" I asked.

"You can say that again!" he added.

"Well, there is another level of learning called emotional learning. Currently, your organization is built on conflict. People fear challenging authority. No offense Bob, but when you say make it happen, no one challenges that command even though they don't know what *it* is." I paused to be sure Bob wasn't going to resist and I could see that he was listening.

I continued, "Ron, your sales people will obediently go through another sales training course. They will try to find new customers, but you run the risk that some of them will quit. They are probably tired of being blamed for the problems. Those that stay, will continue to blame their problems on Manufacturing to justify their existence. The emotional trauma of challenging authority is fear. Fear leads to compliance. Emotional learning is all about changing compliance into commitment."

This is Al. Once again I was scared because Tom challenged Bob's leadership and confronted Ron. No one gets away with making Ron wrong in front of Bob. But it seemed to work. We had broken the dam. The conflict was released. We all left that meeting with a different energy. I realized later that we were finally committed to something rather than in compliance with Bob's command of make it happen.

As always, Ron was "I told you so" about what happened. The conflict came back very quickly. There are times that it is very difficult to like that guy. Whatever the emotional learning level is, it better show up fast. I need to learn to like Ron or it isn't going to work.

That night I told my wife about the meeting. It was similar to the night after my first Swing to Balance lesson. I knew I had found the answer and was excited thinking about the potential for my people. The manufacturing aspects of what Tom had told us were very doable. It would require a lot of coordination with Sales and Engineering. Maybe that is what Swing to Balance means? I then remembered how my hook came back. I went to bed knowing that this is not going to be easy. The only thing I could think was Trust your Swing, daddy. I was like Vijay the night before the last round of the Masters. How do you sleep knowing that tomorrow the pressure will increase?

Chapter 8
Conscious Intention

Many people who play golf have never taken a lesson from a golf professional. They learn to play by going to a golf course and playing. I did it that way

When people learn to play by instinct, they develop a muscle memory of what works and what doesn't, and they tend to repeat the positive patterns of behavior. Within a short period of time, they develop an instinctive pattern of swinging the club that keeps the ball in play. A person with a slice will begin to aim to the left so that the ball will slice back into the fairway. The body and brain are very good a figuring out compensating strategies of hitting the ball.

Millions of golfers use baseball swing mechanics to swing a golf club. Once they hit the ball there is no conscious continuation of the swing. Very quickly they develop the muscle memory of hit the ball in their golf swing, and at that point they are hopelessly condemned to be a bad golfer forever.

The important point is to understand the conscious intention of a golf swing versus the reactive swing of a baseball bat. You must consciously teach yourself to Swing to Balance if you want to play good golf. We see people who play both golf and baseball and the game that suffers is golf.

Most executives began their business careers playing a game called manager. They manage by repeating how they were managed. They learn to play the game of management by being in management meetings and watching how other managers manage. Like golfers, they develop an instinctive pattern of managing people that keeps the company moving ahead and profitable.

There are management development training programs that suggest different ways of managing, but the norm within most companies is to repeat the process used and accepted by the senior managers.

The swing mechanics of management are not the same as the swing mechanics of leadership. They are as different as a baseball swing is from a golf swing. Senior executives are referred to as senior leaders, but most are senior managers. They might know the mechanics of leadership, but their muscle memory is of management.

It was now very obvious from my interaction with Bob, Al, and Ron that I was confronted with baseball players who wanted to be golfers. More accurately, they were all good managers with very limited leadership skill. I never doubted that they knew the term leadership and could tell me what leaders do versus managers, but the instinctive muscle memory of manager behavior was very strong in all three. They knew how to hit the ball, drop the bat, and run.

At this point in our story you need to know that the human resource equivalent of hit the ball means whack the people, drop the blame on others, and run back to the office and hide. The negative feedback mechanics of manager behavior is very well known. In the case of Ron, he would whack on Al, drop the blame on Operations, and hide behind the excuse that the price of the product was too high. He would also whack on his sales people for not making enough calls, drop the blame on Manufacturing, and hide behind the excuse of not enough time or smart enough people. Hit the ball, drop the bat, and run. What a great game!

When people work for a manager like Ron, they instinctively learn to survive the whacking. Like the slicer in golf, they instinctively learn to aim to the left. They learn to shift the blame from themselves to another entity that cannot defend themselves from being whacked. Over time the organization becomes full of blame. Everyone is being whacked and everyone is hiding in their bunker called a functional job description. The cynics claim that the beatings will continue until morale improves.

Bob's command to make it happen was actually a whack on the side of the head for his managers. It was a whack because the implied message was make it happen, stupid. The command to make it happen was followed by dropping the blame on someone, typically Ron and the Sales Department, and hiding out in his office until the next senior managers meeting.

Bob learned this behavior from the Chairman. When the board would meet, they would whack the CEO, drop the blame on the management team, and run to their next meeting.

As a consultant it is easy to see the patterns of the manager game, just like it is easy to see someone trying to hit a golf ball with a baseball swing. In business there is an old saying that, "If you can't stand the heat (the whacking), get out of the kitchen (quit)."

It is a difficult assignment to change this instinctive game. Many businesses fail because of the whacking. The absolute key to successful change is to identify the true cause of the problem. In golf it is the muscle memory of hit the ball, drop the bat and run. In business it is hit the people (numbers), drop the blame and run. This game is deeply imbedded in the Mass Production business model. Successfully changing any organization will not happen by shifting the blame one more time.

During the next several weeks, I had additional discussions with Bob; Rene, the President; and Cheryl Keeting, the Director of Human Resources. Cheryl had conducted leadership and teamwork workshops in the past with little or no success. She was very cynical. I suggested that the past interventions were not wrong, rather that they were conducted in the old context. Fortunately, Bob understood the context thing and made an executive decision to move forward with my recommendations.

We agreed to begin the transformation of Galexey by conducting a three-day leadership workshop for sixteen members of the senior leadership team. The workshop is entitled, "Swing to Balance, Creating Organizational Alignment to Meet the Challenges of the New Business Environment." It includes a Simulation conducted on the golf course. I assured Cheryl and Rene that it was appropriate for golfers and nongolfers alike. Both were very skeptical, thinking it was another chance for the men to do what they wanted to do.

The arrangements were made and the day of the workshop arrived. Five minutes before beginning the workshop, Al let me know that Rene would not be here for the session. She had a personal matter come up that would prevent her from being here.

I figured she would find an excuse to not be here. She was very resistant to Bob's reasoning, I thought. Cheryl was present— she had no choice.

I opened the workshop by saying, "Good morning everyone. I appreciate the opportunity to help you transform the *Business of the BUSINESS* called Galexey Incorporated. The business environment has changed, as we all know. You have responded to that challenge with many very effective strategies and innovative approaches to doing business differently."

I could immediately see the cynics and those who knew that what they had done in the past hadn't worked. It was very important not to patronize them or whack them one more time.

I continued by saying, "The dynamics of the new business environment are unprecedented. Customers are now conditioned to have it their way with speed. As customers, we won't wait in line or tolerate doing our banking only when the banks are open. The ATM machine is open anytime, anywhere, and we are able to customize the transaction the way we want it."

I told them that the potential of this new business model was first revealed in Stanley Davis famous book *Future Perfect* in 1987. In less than ten years the reality of the Internet was transforming the business landscape at an exponential rate. I could tell they had heard this message before.

I then ask, "Let me see the hands of those who have heard of Mass Customization?" Five hands went up. The other ten people just looked at me with a blank stare. I suggested that Mass Customization was beginning to be a dominating business model. Once again the cynics were very conspicuous with their behavior. This included Ron. He had raised his hand, having heard of Mass Customization in our previous meetings. He could not allow himself to not know.

A general discussion of Mass Customization revealed that everyone had experienced Mass Customization, but they were unaware of what it was called. From Windows on your computer, to Dell Computers, a cafeteria, ATM machines, and buying paint—everyone had experienced Mass Customization. There were many examples. I suggested, "The question is not whether Mass Customization exists as a business model, rather are you aware that it is happening."

After that discussion some people began to relax, but many were still not sure what would be expected of them during the workshop.

"It is fair to say that every business in every industry will be confronted by the Mass Customization business model in the future. Your customers are asking for specials but the truth about their requests is that they want it customized their way." I could see several sideways glances at that comment. "Many businesses are quickly developing the muscle memory of this new business model, and Mass Customization will not go away because a management team doesn't want to do it that way. General Motors can no longer tell us we have to buy a car the way they want to make it. We now have many choices. So the challenge for General Motors is to adapt the factory to meet the customers demands. The customer is now in charge."

Ariel, the manager of customer service, raised her hand and said, "We have a difficult time with specials. It takes a long time to process the orders, get the parts from the vendors, make the software modifications, and build the units. Then we can't track the costs and have trouble giving management accurate month-end figures. Are you suggesting that we should do more specials?"

Her confrontational tone gave relief to several others in the room. It is always easier to kill the messenger rather than embrace change.

I responded by saying, "Ariel, your point is a good one. Within the business model that currently operates within Galexey, specials are not welcomed by anyone. We are here for the next three days to consider the options. If you are losing customers because you resist specials, maybe you should consider an alternate business model."

The tension was relieved when Bob said, "We must change the current thinking in the company about specials. That's why we are here for three days. Tom will be helping us evaluate the options and consider how we should change."

Bob went on to tell the group of his conversation with another CEO who had encountered the same situation and how he had resolved the problem. His comments were good, but the tension remained. Actually, the resistance increased as everyone expected the make it happen command from Bob.

I continued the opening remarks by saying, "Now that we are aware of Mass Customization, we could easily approach this situation with a make it happen command." I watched everyone wince in fear. "But I've suggested to Bob that we need to take time to really understand what *it* is before we begin another search for the solution."

This was a risky statement to make, but I had prepared Bob for it. There was an immediate response by some people, especially those who worked for Al. They were shocked that anyone could challenge Bob's make it happen command.

Al instinctively spoke, "We've been talking with Tom for six weeks now about our situation. In the beginning, I thought he was crazy, but I had the benefit of working with Tom on my golf swing and it is amazing what can happen if we all learn to Swing to Balance."

This statement made no sense to most people even though the theme for the workshop was Swing to Balance. We weren't to that point in the opening remarks.

"Thanks Al for that vote of confidence in the Swing to Balance process, but I'm sure there are many people who would like to know what that means and how it will impact them over the next three days. I'm sure this is especially true for those of you who do not play golf," I added.

I could see the nods of agreement with that statement and Ariel blurted out, "I hate golf. It's a stupid game. If we're going to spend three day learning how to play golf, you're crazy!"

I could see her anger and Ariel was not alone in her feelings. The bunkers were full of nongolfers. In golf language, a bunker is another term for sand trap. People dig into their bunkers to resist the onslaught of any change initiative. It happens every day in every organization. It is a common Mass Production business model tactic. Whack the people, blame someone else, and hide in your bunker. If your bunker is well built, it will protect you from the blame being thrown around in the organization.

"Ariel, I can understand your concern about golf, and I'm sure all the nongolfers feel the same way. I assure you we aren't going to spend three days learning to play golf. We are here to consider the challenge of change confronting Galexey. We will go to the golf course tomorrow to learn how to play a game that some of us hate. Many of you hate specials, but you may need to learn to play the specials game to survive. Every company in every industry is being challenged to learn to play a new game that they have not played before."

I could see a curious look on some faces now and I continued, "When the game changes, it doesn't matter that you are the best player in the old game. Once the old game becomes obsolete, you are out of business. In that context, Galexey is the best player at building standard units. But the new game requires that you build specials with the same ability. You can no longer tell customers to accept what you want to build because it is the only game you know. You must learn the new game or be gone. You may hate the new game, but you need to learn to enjoy it if you are going to be successful."

"What if your wrong?" Jill asked. Jill was the CFO and a very bright person. "There is a lot of risk in changing the way we do business. We've been very successful for a long time," she added.

"That's a good question, Jill. I could be wrong. That's why we are going to take three days to consider all the possibilities before we decide to change anything. We are going to simulate changing the game before we do anything for real. The astronauts simulated going to the moon before they decided to risk their lives. The simulation will give you the experience from which to judge the risk," I added.

Jill was not satisfied by the answer and I could see the same tension in several other people. It is very normal to have fear when confronted with change. It's easier to whack the consultant, drop the blame on the Sales Department, and hide out in your bunker. The muscle memory of the old game is comfortable.

It was obvious that the management team of Galexey was going to stretch its awareness in the next three days. There isn't any level of pre-workshop communication that can prepare a group for what is going to happen to them on the golf course. I had covered this potential with Bob and Al before the session. Bob had written a memo describing the process, but nothing prepares you for the stark reality that you're here and we're going forward. The first step of transformational change is always to resist the need to change. The muscle memory of the old game is comfortable and as Jill said, "It has worked for years. Why change?" The change agent could be wrong.

This is Al. For the first time in a long time I really enjoyed myself. I was not the one being whacked. I was excited to begin the Swing to Balance experience. I understood where Ariel was coming from. I had worked with her for five years now and she was not one of my favorite people. She was always whacking us in Manufacturing about shipping schedules for specials. I was glad she was going to have a tough time for the next three days.

I had talked to my managers. They were fully informed and rather excited about the Simulation. Little did I know what Tom had in store for me? Wait till you find out what he did to me.

Chapter 9
Learning to Learn

"It sounds like you're being critical of how Engineering handles specials. Why wasn't I prepared for this criticism?" asked Ralph.

Ralph was the vice president of Engineering. He had been the heart of the company for years. Fortunately Bob spoke up saying, "Ralph, you were on vacation when we decided to hold this session. There was a very narrow time slot when we could all do this and we made the decision to proceed. We aren't criticizing anything or any department. We are not here because there is anything wrong with the way we do things today. We just need to consider different alternatives, then decide whether the way we currently do things is the most economical way for the future," Bob said.

"That sounds good, but Ron and Al have been nagging us for years about specials. Now it appears you have hired a consultant to tell us how to run Engineering. We've had too many consultants. That IT conversion still doesn't work," Ralph complained.

This is the whacking, blame, hide out process in action and Ralph is one of the biggest offenders.

Sharon, one of Ralph's senior engineers said, "Ralph, I talked with Tom about this session when you were on vacation and it is not about a new way to do specials. It is about a new business model called Mass Customization and how it will challenge us to think different. At least we'll get to play golf," she said.

I had to take charge and did by saying, "Let's step back and review the purpose of the session. Ralph, I apologize for the short notice and the inability to let you know about the purpose of the session, but I thought that Sharon and your senior engineers would have had an opportunity to talk to you before today."

"I just got back yesterday and bang, I'm here," Ralph said.

"We'll let that be a leadership point during our discussions. Frequently, there isn't time to inform all the key stakeholders to a situation and they arrive at the venue of change without notice. This is inevitable and a very important part of our learning experience for the next three days. Decisions must be made and everyone needs to learn to trust the motives and intent of the total group," I suggested.

I moved to a flip chart and put ***Learn to Trust the total group to make intelligent decisions*** on a piece of paper. "We'll build a list from our discussions so we can refer to them later."

"We've made hundreds of lists in the past. Nothing happens from the lists," Ariel asserted. "Are we going to do something about the lists this time?"

Ariel was still cynical about past processes and for good reason. I assured her, "Ariel, we've all done the list building exercises before. We will not leave this conference without a decision on what to do about the things on the list."

"Yeah, we'll probably decide to make it happen, right?" she said.

There was silence. She had hit the nerve ending for everyone. Bob laughed and said, "I promise you, I will never say that again. Tom told me that make it happen isn't an effective leadership command, so we're here to develop a new command."

I put **Learn new leadership commands** on the flip chart. Then I added, **Learn to tell the truth**, and I said, "Ariel just spoke the truth about the command make it happen. We all have our commands that we use to keep people from asking for answers. Have your children ever asked you why something is the way it is?" I asked. "Why do they have to clean their plate or go to bed on time? The most common answer is because I said so. That isn't the real reason, but we would rather use our authority to command than our ability to influence," I suggested.

I wrote **Learn to Influence effectively** on the flip chart.

"Looks like we're in for a lot of learning."

My back was turned so I wasn't sure who made the comment. I turned and asked, "That's a great observation, who said that?"

"I did." It was a middle-aged man named Wally. His name tent said he was manager of Software Development.

"Wally, you are very observant. We are here to learn how to learn a new game. It will require that we learn new skills. We will need to learn to let go of old ways of doing things in order to embrace the new."

I added **Learn to learn** and **Learn to let go** to the list on the flip chart.

"What if some people don't want to learn and some people can't let go?" Wally asked.

"Then we'll help them learn to make choices that serve them well," I responded.

I added **Learn to make choices** to the list.

"We only have three days," Wally added. "Knowing some of the people in this room, you should have schedule this for two weeks."

Everyone laughed and someone said, "There you go again, Wally." I didn't see who made that comment and little did I know what they meant by it. It was obvious that the resistance to learning in the room was strong. They had all been in their bunkers for a long time.

"We aren't going to do the learning organization thing again, are we?" The question came from Bryan, one of Al's managers.

"Can you explain what you mean by that question?" I asked.

Bryan explained how the Operations managers had attended a seminar called the Learning Organization. It was a Peter Senge concept from his famous book, *The Fifth Discipline*. "We all know the Covey stuff also," he added.

"Now that you are all feeling the tension of what we are going to do and what we are going to learn, let me tell you what is going to happen during the next three days." I finally had their attention.

"We are going to spend the rest of today understanding the nature of change and how to learn new skills if change requires that we play a new game. We will talk specifically about your company and your real-life situations. This will not be a theoretical discussion. Tomorrow we will be on the golf course all day learning to play a game some of you have never played before. For those who have played golf, like Ron and Al, you will be challenged to learn to play in a new way."

I finished the introduction and expectations phase of the meeting in the next ten minutes and we took a break. It was now 10:00 a.m. Wally approached me and said, "I hope you didn't think I was being negative."

"You weren't being negative. You were telling the truth and expressing legitimate concerns that other people in the room also have and are unwilling to voice at this time. Frankly, I appreciate your willingness to challenge the process. That's the first step in moving from compliance to commitment."

Wally looked at me, not knowing how to respond and said, "Well we've tried many times to tell Bob and Ron, and Al for that matter, that we should stop doing specials. Specials are killing Ariel's customer service representatives and they are very time consuming for my software engineers, but they won't listen. They think our people can just work overtime and get it done. I'm going to lose some people if we don't start treating them like humans," he added.

I looked at Wally and said, "The business model of Mass Production treats many operative people like things, or objects, or resources." I walked toward the flip chart and added *Learn to treat people like people.* "When we come back from the break we'll tell everyone what we added, is that fair?" I asked. Wally agreed and walked away. I could tell he really wanted things to change.

I started toward the restroom and ran into Al. "That was a tough beginning," he said. "Remember, I warned you about Wally."

"Yes. He'll be okay," I said. The restroom was buzzing. I heard someone say, "I can't believe he said that." I wasn't sure whether they were talking about me, but it was a good sign that the truth was coming out.

As I washed my hands, I looked in the mirror and Bob was standing behind me waiting to say something. He said, "This is going to be great. We've never had a meeting where we could tell the truth. I wish the Chairman was here."

"Call him. There's still time, and we definitely could use one more player now that Rene can't be here," I suggested.

"Do you think he would intimidate the people?" Bob asked.

"Not this group. Now that you've let go, I think they will be free to experience change."

"I'll call him," Bob said and he left.

Why is it we fear people in authority. Why does Bob fear that the Chairman will intimidate people? Is the Chairman perceived to be a leader or a dictator? He's probably a nice guy who is hitting balls I thought.

As we reassembled there was a new energy in the room. It was much more relaxed. Somehow a break always relieves the tension. People have a chance to talk privately with a friend and they conclude that it is going to be okay.

I started by saying, "At the break, Wally and I talked about another concern he had and we added an item to our learning list, ***Learn to treat people like people.*** If you have any Learn To items to add to the list, either openly or in private, please suggest them. We are here to learn many things. Please make sure your agenda is met."

"For the next hour we are going to talk about the three forms of learning and how we are going to experience learning in the workshop." I directed them to open section one of the participant guide that was prepared for the session.

I started the discussion by saying, "Page one makes reference to three forms of learning. They are

1.   Knowledge learning

2.   Emotional learning

3.   Physical learning.

"It also says, adults learn from experience and they aren't good at it."

The page contained examples of each form of learning. I then turned to Al and said, "Quickly relate the story to the group of that day on the driving range when you first encountered Swing to Balance. We'll then use that example to extract the three learning processes."

My request caught Al a little off guard but he easily agreed. He wanted everyone to know all the details, and that they were in for a treat tomorrow. I warned him by saying, "Al, it was a great experience for you because you were a student ready for the lesson. Remember some people are here and aren't looking for a golf lesson. It may be a totally different experience for many people."

Ariel said, "Yeah Al. Remember I hate golf!"

Everyone laughed, but she was still not convinced she was going to the golf course. She could still find an excuse not to participate.

I then suggested we break Al's Swing to Balance story down into the three learning realms. "Did Al know about Swing to Balance?" I asked.

"Yes, he had watched the Swing to Balance video that you had given him two years before," someone suggested.

"He knows about Swing to Balance." And I checked knowledge learning on a flip chart.

"Did he have emotional learning about golf?" I asked. People weren't sure how to answer, but I suggested, "Think about how he was feeling as he was hitting balls one last time before quitting the game."

"That's the way I feel every Friday," Mark, one of the sales people responded. "I go home every week feeling defeated and I feel like I'm starting all over every Monday. You people ought to be in Sales for a week and you'd know what emotional learning is."

Everyone laughed, but Mark was serious. "You can laugh but it's real. If we don't address this specials thing, I'm going to lose my biggest account and the emotions of that experience will not be pretty."

"Mark's right," I added. "We all have learned to manage our emotions, but there comes a time in every work experience where we can't handle it any longer. This is especially true in sales," I added.

"Are there other examples of emotional learning in Al's story?" I asked.

"I'm not sure about Al's experience, but I was terrified this morning when you confronted Bob with the make it happen thing," Sharon said.

"That's a great example of emotional learning," I suggested. "We learn to fear the boss and tolerate the fear. That's emotional learning," I added.

"What would life be like without a little fear of authority?" Bob added. "It gets you going in the morning."

"Maybe for you, but it doesn't do much for me," Al volunteered.

There was silence for a moment then someone said, "Now the truth is coming out."

"Al, tell them more specifically how I changed your physical learning mechanism during the Swing to Balance lesson."

"Tom put me in the Balanced Finish position and held me there. He told me to feel my body in that position," Al said. "At first it felt very strange," he added.

"We will use physical learning tomorrow on the driving range. When you are trying to change a physical behavior, you must put your body in the new position and feel how it feels. This is called changing the muscle memory of the old game. We'll talk about it in more detail later. For now, I want you to realize that some things cannot be learned by telling people about them. You must physically do them to learn. This is very common in playing the piano, for example. You cannot learn to play the piano by merely reading the music. You must play the scales over and over to train you fingers how to play the notes on the page."

"That's true in learning to play the guitar," someone added.

"It is true in everything we do. A surgeon can know all there is to know about heart surgery, but he or she must sooner or later train their muscle memory to do the operations. And there is a lot of emotional learning in the medical profession," I added.

I could see that the people were now engaged. Almost everyone volunteered a significant learning experience from the past and quickly categorized it in one of the three forms. It became very obvious that the three realms were linked together.

"The important point for our consideration the next two days is to understand the different learning processes associated with organizational change. Tomorrow, some of you will experience the emotional trauma of having to perform without having a well developed muscle memory," I suggested.

I told them a very quick account of Vijay Singh winning the Masters and how his son told him, *Trust your Swing, daddy.* I gave the example of a person in a spelling bee who knows how to spell a word but might get it wrong because of the emotional fear of failure.

"Most organizational change initiatives don't fail for lack of knowledge. Executives know about teamwork, empowerment, partnering and all the requirements of the new business environment. They don't need to learn to know more. Initiatives fail because executives fear letting go of authority to those who must execute the commands, and those who must execute the commands have no muscle memory of the new behavior," I suggested.

Once again there was silence. Some people were trying to process my statements, but most had just realized why Galexey had failed to change in the past. It would have been very easy to activate the whacking mechanism at that time.

I finished the discussion on the learning processes by saying, "Tomorrow you will experience all three learning realms. It will be very different for those who have played golf and those who hate golf. The important thing is to value the learning mode of your playing partners and use the correct commands for the situation."

Little did they know at this point what learning to learn would mean to them by the end of the session. By then they would value the process of learning differently.

This is Al. I was silent at this point. I was terribly aware of what happened to me before, during, and after the Swing to Balance lesson. I could recall the depressed state I was in about golf. I could recall the exhilaration I had after the lesson. I realized that the change I experienced had nothing to do with knowing anything different. It was all physical and emotional learning.

I was now starting to think about why our company couldn't digest the specials. We know how to do them. We just don't want to do them. It's all about emotions, I think. Stay tuned, it gets more interesting.

Chapter 10
Betting the Company

We broke for lunch and Bob let me know that the Chairman could not make it for today's session, but he would be able to play golf tomorrow.

"We aren't going to play golf in the same context that he knows as golf. We're going to play business on the golf course tomorrow," I said.

"What do you want me to tell him? Should he come out?" Bob asked.

"Sure, if you want to be his coach," I suggested. "How good of a golfer is he?"

"He's a 12 handicap.. Plays almost every day that ends in Y," Bob laughed. "He has played all over the world. He tries to play all the great courses. There's probably nothing you or I can teach him," Bob suggested.

He's a 12 handicap and there is nothing to learn. What does that tell you? I thought.

"That may be true," I suggested. "I'm hungry let's eat."

I could tell that Bob really wanted the Chairman to attend the session. As we were walking toward the lunch area I said, "Ask him to be on time. We'll start in the seminar room promptly at 8:00. If he's late, he will not be able to play."

Bob lagged behind, so I decided to sit beside Ralph. I asked if he was saving the seat for anyone and he motioned for me to sit down.

"How long have you been doing this?" Ralph asked.

"By this, if you mean leadership and golf, about eighteen years," I said.

"Really. You seem very relaxed and confident of what you are doing. Doesn't it bother you when people ask those confrontational questions?" he asked.

"Not at all. If I were in your shoes, I'd ask the same questions. You are entitled to know what is going to happen and why we are doing what we are doing," I suggested.

Sharon was across the table and said, "We need to put three additional Learn Tos on the list."

"What are they?" I asked.

"Learn to listen, Learn to be patient, and Learn to keep your promises," she said. "Do those fit into what we'll be learning tomorrow?" she asked.

"We'll add them to the list and you can tell me whether they are important after golf tomorrow. I think they fit, but it is more important for you to determine that for yourself," I added.

"What if I don't have any golf clubs?" Tina asked.

"That's okay. We have arranged for rental clubs for those who indicated they need clubs. Did you put your name on the need clubs list?" I asked.

"I'm not sure."

"We'll check the list after lunch," I said.

"Tina, what do you do at Galexey?" I asked.

Ralph answered the question, "Tina works with all our vendors. She buys right."

"How long have you done that?" I asked Tina.

Once again Ralph answered, "Forever. She's our employee of the decade."

I could see a pattern of behavior in Ralph that is very common at the senior level. He would not let his people answer questions for themselves. This is a control mechanism. I knew right then that Ralph was going to have a very difficult time on the golf course tomorrow.

I tried one more time by asking Tina a question that Ralph couldn't answer. "Tina, I take it you don't play golf?"

"I played when I was in high school, but I haven't played in the past twenty years. I have five children and there isn't time for golf in our family," she said

There was a twinge in her comment about time for golf that seemed strange, but I let it drop by saying, "Well, I hope you enjoy the process tomorrow."

Tina said, "I can't wait."

It is amazing how people anticipate situations. I could tell there was an agenda within the engineering group that had not yet been identified. The lunch break is not the time to create tension, so I started to eat and dropped the subject of golf or any reference to tomorrow's happenings.

Bob tapped me on the shoulder and said, "The Chairman will be here in the morning. He wanted to know, what's the bet?" Bob laughed.

"The company," I said.

"What's that mean?" Ralph asked with a sideways glance.

"Some people bet the farm. Tomorrow we're going to bet the future of the company," I said.

Sharon quickly said, "We better add *Learn to bet wisely* to the list. Betting our future sound like big stakes," she said.

"The stakes are large," I added. "You will have some big money at stake tomorrow and you will need to think carefully about your wagers."

"You mean there is money involved and I have to play with rental clubs?" Tina asked.

"There is still time for you to get another set," I suggested.

"Are we playing for real money?" Mike asked. I nodded affirmative. "Then we'll have to tolerate Ron," he added.

Mike had been quiet all morning and until now at lunch. I asked him what he did at Galexey and he said he was the manager of Accounting and reported to Jill.

Ralph added, "Ron is a big time gambler on the course. He'll figure out the bet and intimidate everyone. He's a good player. Wait till you see him hit that new driver he has. When he hits it straight, it goes a mile."

"So he's a hit the ball man. Is that right?" I asked.

Ralph wasn't sure what to say, but Sharon quickly confirmed, "You got that right."

It was shaping up to be a fantastic learning experience for everyone. Little did they know what was going to happen to them on the golf course tomorrow. Speculation traveled fast about the money.

Mark yelled from another table, "Hey Tom. Do we get to keep the money if we win?"

"Sure. That's the game. But you might lose the company if you lose," I added.

"Sounds like we better add some learning stuff to the list," Tina suggested.

"Like what?" asked Mike.

"Like how to understand the rules of the game before we charge off thinking we know how to win. I smell something fishy here," Tina suggested.

Ralph said, "Tina, you've been working with vendors too long. You're always smelling something fishy."

"That's what I get paid to do," she said confidently and she got up and left.

The suspense was building nicely. Everyone was speculating about tomorrow. The bets were being placed on Ron.

I heard Ariel say, "This isn't fair. No one can beat Ron. I don't even play golf."

I could hear the anger in her comment, so I suggested, "He'll have to Swing to Balance to win. Ask him if he knows what that means? Maybe he doesn't have an advantage. I'll give you a clue. His new driver won't help him on the last hole," I said.

I had to check with my office before we reconvened the afternoon session. I excused myself and went back to the seminar room to get my cell phone. Wally followed me and when we were out of range from the others, he asked, "Something strange is going to happen tomorrow on the golf course, isn't it?"

"You are very perceptive, Wally," I confirmed.

"We're going to bet the company and people like me who have never played golf before are going to participate. That is strange." And he walked away saying, "This will either be a disaster or a real learning experience."

This is Al. I didn't hear the lunch conversation, but word traveled fast that we were going to have a big bet on the golf course tomorrow. I laughed to myself because Tom had told me a little about the golf course experience when we were trying to decide whether to do this thing or not. I was not aware that there was a bet or money involved, but Tom had told me that the nongolfers would not be at a disadvantage. I was sure, knowing Tom, that there was something fishy going on and that his comment about Ron had some significance, but at this point, my excitement was growing. I could see the people beginning to relax and enjoy the process.

I was very concerned when I heard that the Chairman was coming. He's a nice guy, but not everyone knows him that way. His salary is public information and a lot of people think he gets paid a lot of money to be playing golf all over the world. People resent that especially when we made some budget cuts recently.

Oh well. Tom agreed that he could participate. I guess it will be okay. I just hope I don't have to be in his foursome.

Chapter 11
The Need for Vision

I added the ***Learn to listen, Learn to be patient, Learn to keep promises,*** and ***Learn to bet wisely*** to the flip chart as Sharon had suggested. I also added ***Learn the rules of the game before playing*** as Tina had suggested. We hadn't talked about some of these issues yet, so these learning items would be a nice beginning to the afternoon session.

The participants began to wander in as the time for reconvening approached. The energy in the room was different. Things were much more relaxed. I could hear joking and laughter about the golf. I could hear Ron bragging about his foursome.

Evidently, he had already selected his team.

I started by saying, "Welcome back. We have some good news to announce. Bob, why don't you tell them who will be joining us tomorrow?" I asked.

The invitation caught Bob by surprise, but told the group, "The Chairman, Frank Shamanski, will be joining us for golf. He is an avid golfer, as many of you know. I asked Tom if he thought it would intimidate us, and he said it wouldn't. So I invited him to be with us. He just might learn something," Bob said jokingly.

"Let's add ***Learn to be humble*** to our learning list for him," Sharon said.

"Wow, the truth serum really got to you didn't it?" noted Wally.

"As long as we're studying leadership, he might as well get something out of this too," Sharon added.

I moved to the flip chart and added ***Learn to be humble.*** "Any others?" I asked.

"We need to learn to say no," said Kathy. "We take on too many projects and can't possibly get them done."

Kathy was in the IT group and knew the trauma of overload. I asked, "Can you give us an example of when you should say no?"

"Do you have all day?" she cynically asked. "You've heard from everyone how the IT conversion isn't working. It isn't our fault. No one wants it to happen. Every manager wants us to do it to someone else, rather their group. Al doesn't want his group to be affected. Now he wants me to learn to play golf."

I could see Kathy's anger and it was justified. I suggested, "We have three days to understand leading Galexey into the future. I'm sure everyone is overloaded and feels frustrated about getting things accomplished. I feel that way in my business every week. We all need to learn to prioritize our work differently. Is that what you mean by learning to say no?" I asked.

"Yes, but there is more to it than prioritizing the work. We know our priorities. We just have too many priorities," she said.

Everyone laughed, but I could tell it was a false laugh. Kathy was angered by the laughter and said, "You all can laugh. We're here wasting three days playing golf. The conversion will be three weeks behind because of this. Our time is more valuable than playing golf all the time like the Chairman and you Ron," Kathy angrily added.

Kathy looked at Bob and said, "I'm sorry. I shouldn't have said that about the Chairman."

Her comment slipped out in the anger and I could tell she felt very guilty. I looked at the group and said, "This is an example of why we are here. Kathy has told the truth about how she feels. It is not an easy feeling to express. If it comes out when we're angry, we feel guilty for saying what we are feeling."

"But we all know it's true," Bob added. "Kathy, I know what you said is on the minds of many people in the room. You don't need to apologize."

I picked up from Bob's comment and said, "We need to learn how to link priorities to something so that we don't have too many priorities. This is a very important leadership skill." I turned to the flip chart and added *Learn to link priorities to vision* to the list.

"What if we don't have a vision?" Sharon asked.

"That's what we are going to talk about this afternoon," I suggested.

Without stopping for breath I said, "Open your participant guide to the second section entitled Leadership." I waited a moment while they reshuffled the books and papers and were on the right page. I then continued, "Leadership, like golf is an overtaught subject. How many of you have been to a leadership seminar before today?" Every hand went up.

"We've all been through the *Seven Habits*," Al added.

"What is the first habit?" I asked the group. There was silence. "The *Seven Habits* is an excellent leadership offering from Steven Covey Institute. I know people who have been completely transformed from that workshop. On the other hand, I know many people who have attended that workshop who can't tell me the first habit. Who remembers the first habit?" I asked again.

Only two hands went up. "This is why I suggest that subjects like leadership and golf are overtaught and underlearned. There is a big difference between being taught and having learned the game. Our knowing self knows about math, language, management, leadership, and yes golf. On the subject of leadership, we generally know the habits that make great leaders. I'm sure we could make another list." I looked at Ariel and she returned an exasperated nod.

"We need to translate the seven habits into behavior. In other words, we need to make the habits of leadership our own habits. A habit is a form of muscle memory. Tomorrow, we will learn to convert knowledge into behavior," I said.

"Don't we do that at times?" Ralph asked. "We did an assessment of the habits using a 360 feedback instrument and found that we in fact do many of the *seven habits*."

"Yeah, and we found that we don't do them very well. Our total score was below 40 percent. Remember!" added Cheryl. Cheryl was the Human Resource person who conducted the 360 assessment.

There was an angry tone in Cheryl's voice. She added, "To me the *Seven Habits* leadership training was a high priority, but to you it was not linked to anything. You guys acted as if it was a waste of time, just like some of you are acting right now. Here we go again talking about leadership. We've talked about leadership for five years and nothing has changed. I like the comment Tom made earlier, we've accepted our handicap," she added.

She seemed to direct her anger at Bob and Ron, but it sounded like a universal condemnation of the entire group.

"Cheryl is right," I said. "The same scenario plays out every day in hundreds of organizations. The need for a new form of leadership is increasing exponentially. The ability to learn leadership is declining rapidly. Let's be very clear what I mean by that. Leadership is being taught in thousands of seminars like the *Seven Habits* workshop you attended. Leadership is not being learned and applied. It's like golf. Thousands of people take golf lessons every day and their handicap doesn't improve. The question we must ask and answer is why?"

"Well, why is it?" Ron asked. "Do you know?" he added in a confrontational tone.

I could feel the challenge in Ron's question. "That's why we're here, Ron. To examine the gap between knowing about leadership and doing what leaders do. I'm sure you have it in your sales people. They know they should call on new accounts, but they continue to do what's comfortable. The same is true in golf, as we will find out tomorrow," I added.

Ron nodded in agreement and before he could ask a follow-up question I said, "Turn to the next page in your participant guide." On that page was a description of the three forms of learning we had identified earlier. "The key to changing behavior is to program the muscle memory system with the behavior we want. Said another way, if you want to swing like Tiger Woods, you must program your muscles to feel the way he feels when he swings. Another example would be learning to ride a bike. You must get on and ride to train yourself to balance."

"Isn't that risky?" Tina asked.

"Potentially yes," I responded. "It depends on the consequences of failure. We can fall off the bike and get hurt. That's why we provide training wheels to help a child at first, and we will provide training wheels for you on the golf course tomorrow. No one will get hurt, I promise," I laughed.

I quickly continued the discussion by saying, "In the world of business today, the consequences of failure to change are enormous. The seven habits are known. But the first habit, *Start with the End in Mind,* has not been built into the muscle memory of most executives. *Start with the End in Mind* requires a vision of the end, but most executives are visionless."

"They think they have a vision," Cheryl added. "They think it's the people who can't see the big picture."

"You're right," I confirmed. "Let's see why that is. Turn to the next page," I said.

We were beginning to track the process that was a part of the participant guide. On the next page were the words

Vision
Mission
Purpose
Objective
Goals
Strategy
Measurements
Expectations.

"Take a moment and write a brief definition of each word as you currently define it. There is nothing right or wrong with any definition, so take two minutes and write something down beside each word," I suggested.

I slowly walked around the room to see if people were writing on the page. Many people were just looking at the words.

"You can't think words on to the page. Write something opposite each word. If you don't know a definition, write don't know," I instructed. Having to write something on a page in a workbook creates tension for many people. They believe that someone is going to check their answers and they don't like to reveal the fact that they don't have an accurate definition for a commonly used term. For those who still weren't sure why they were here, refusing to write was a sign of resistance.

I could see several people who were refusing to write on the page. One person by the name of Brad had his arms crossed and was sitting back as if he had finished. I walked over to see his page and he turned it just as I arrived. His name tent said Legal on it. He was the corporate attorney. Al had warned me about Legal.

After the two minutes, I suggested we would let the collective intelligence in the room define the terms. This was the first time I had used the term collective intelligence so I suggested, "Tomorrow, on the golf course you will learn to value the collective intelligence of your group. It may be a new way for you to think about teamwork." I looked at Brad and intentionally called on him to tell us what he had written as the definition for vision.

"It all semantics," he responded.

"Can you tell me what you mean by semantics?" I asked.

"Vision, mission, strategy, goals, they all mean the same thing," he said.

"And that is?" I asked.

Brad was very irritated and defended his statement by saying, "In a court of law you would need to be very accurate in what you mean by these terms and several of them are semantical," he asserted in a confident legal tone.

"I totally agree, Brad. We need to be accurate. How would you define vision to a judge?" I asked.

Once again he resisted by saying, "That depends on the case and the situation," increasing the resistance in the tone of his voice.

"He's not going to be in my foursome tomorrow," said Mark.

Everyone laughed and Brad got very mad. "You guys always laugh at the legal perspective, but without our work you would all be in jail. There are many legally correct definitions for these words. It's all semantics," Brad continued the argument by sarcastically asking me, "How do you define vision?"

"Let's see what everyone wrote before I tell you what I think it is. What did the rest of you write?" I asked.

"Vision is what you want to be," said Cheryl. "It's like the picture on the box of a puzzle," she added. "Without the picture of what the puzzle will look like when it's finished, you can't put the puzzle together."

"That's a great way to think about vision," I said.

"What if you were given a puzzle and told to put it together as a team, and the Chairman wouldn't give you the box top." The question came from Bryan. He went on to say, "We've been doing teams in the Operations group for three years now, and I can tell you we have no clue as to what's on the box top."

I could see Al bristle at Bryan's comment, but his anger was quickly relieved when Bob said, "The title on the puzzle in my office is *Snow Storm*. All the pieces are white. That's one reason I invited the Chairman to be with us tomorrow," he added.

We defined the words in terms of questions that need to be answered every day as people do the work of any business. Some people quickly realized the answers were on the next page of the participant guide. The answers were

Vision	"What we want to become?"
Mission/Purpose	"Why we exist?"
Goals/Objectives	"What action steps lead to the Vision?"
Strategy	"How will we deploy resources?"
Measurements	"How will we know we are winning?"
Expectations	"How will we know we will be satisfied with the results?"

"Do you think these definitions would be accepted by the judge, Brad?" I asked. Brad was still brooding about his rebuff by the group. He just glared at me and remained silent. *He'll be a real challenge on the golf course,* I thought.

"These are a few of the questions that people ask every day when they go to work. If they know the answers, they will work efficiently, effectively, and effortlessly. If they can't answer the question, they will make up an answer to fit their own needs. If the answer appears to be wrong, they will withdraw in silence for fear of making a mistake," I suggested. "And as Brad points out, some people think it's all semantics."

"Simply stated, the role of leadership is to answer questions for people so that the organization can function. You will need to answer many of these questions tomorrow to function properly. The question for you to consider tonight is who will answer these questions for you. You may ask them and not receive and answer. Or you may forget to ask the question and find out later that you should have asked. There are many possibilities. The Simulation will help you feel, not just know about, the importance of these answers."

There was silence. People weren't sure what they had been told and they didn't know how to respond. I said, "With that let's take a break."

Al came up and said, "That was tough."

"What was tough?" I asked.

"The argument with Brad. I told you he was hard to convince. He's always that way."

"Lawyers are trained to think that way and we better be glad they are. The legal aspects of business and life are very precise," I suggested. "I once conducted the Simulation for a group of lawyers. They are nice people when you get them on the golf course, but they are tough when fulfilling their job at work."

"Do you think Brad will participate tomorrow?" Al asked.

"He'll be fine," I suggested. "He'll be fine."

"How do you know that?" Al asked.

"The rules of golf are very precise," I said. "He'll be fine."

This is Al. If tomorrow changes how Legal thinks, it will be a miracle. It will never happen. Those people are the anchors of the world. If we did business strictly by what Legal said, we would never do business. You have to break the rules sometimes to get things done.

All of a sudden I was concerned about what I had just said. Tomorrow, we were going to play a game that has a very precise set of rules, and the pros play the game strictly by the rules. It can't be true that we will have to work the way Legal dictates. I wanted to go ask Tom, but he was on the phone.

I then thought about what Bob had said about the Snow Storm and the Chairman. I needed to ask Bob if he was sure he wanted the Chairman to be here tomorrow. Someone might embarrass him by asking him for a vision?

I was mad about what Bryan had said. We had a vision for the team initiative. I wonder why he couldn't see it. Then I wondered why he hadn't said anything about it before. My gut was starting to churn. Stay tuned.

Chapter 12
The Potential of No Conflict

It was now 3:00 p.m. and people were getting tired of the intellectual challenge. The last section on the difference between vision, purpose, strategy and measurements was mentally taxing. It is much easier for people to trust their muscle memory and do it the old way. If a vision doesn't exist in the executive suite, why should people below them be concerned? That's not their job.

Since the Chairman is coming tomorrow, I decided to switch the agenda for the last hour and deal with the competitive advantage issue. When the board or chairman level of an organization are involved in a Swing to Balance Simulation, I like to make sure that the case for change has a high-level strategic connection. The senior leaders must be certain that the competitive advantage of the organization can be sustained into the future, and, if not, how does it need to change. Discussion of this issue is a killer from an intellectual standpoint, but we need to do it in the next hour.

As we reconvened, I asked, "Are there any questions about what we've covered so far?"

Ariel raised her hand and said, "I don't want to appear stupid, but what does vision and purpose and all this stuff have to do with golf? Do we need a vision to participate tomorrow?"

"Good question," I replied.

Before I could answer, Ron blurted out, "The entire game of golf is about vision and strategy."

The tone of his voice implied, "You're stupid for not knowing that." Ron had been rather quiet all day. He was confident he would be the top dog tomorrow. Everyone was building him up to be the pre-Simulation favorite to win the money. That made him feel cocky.

Ariel isn't shy and said, "See what I mean. I said I didn't want to be called stupid for not knowing, Ron. I have no idea how to play golf. If I'm going to play, I want to be prepared. It would be nice if you guys in Sales were a little considerate once in a while."

I intervened and said, "Ron, why don't you give Ariel an example of the importance of vision in golf and in sales?"

"In golf you have to visualize the shot before every swing. You have to gauge the wind, the distance, and where you want the ball to land. You have to be able to see the line of a putt before you hit it. If you can't read greens you're dead. In sales --," Ron thought for a moment. Everyone could see that he didn't have a quick answer. Then he said, "You have to plan your time and territory and be able to develop accounts."

"Sounds like you're confusing vision and strategy," Ariel asserted.

"How so?" Ron challenged.

"If I get vision, it's the picture on the box. It has nothing to do with time. When you start managing time, that's strategy, how you will deploy resources, right?" Ariel looked at me for confirmation and help in the battle with Ron.

I said, "She's right. Time is a deployment issue, not a vision issue."

I directed my comment to the entire group hoping to stop the battle between Ron and Ariel, but Ron would not let go. He retorted, "That might be so, but sales is all about vision. My people better have a vision of their territory being penetrated or they're in trouble."

"Now you're mixing vision and measurements," Ariel asserted. "No wonder we're having sales problems. Market penetration is a measure not a vision, right?" Once again she looked at me for confirmation.

"How long are we going to have to listen to these guys fight?" asked Tina. "Let's get on with the show."

"I won't let them fight much longer. They're going to be partners on the course tomorrow. Ariel can explain it to him tomorrow." I laughed and continued, "It is, however, very important to realize how easy it is to confuse these issues. For this reason, we need to define the vision, purpose, goals and strategies for Galexey after Ron and Ariel accurately understand the differences on the course tomorrow."

"Why is this so hard to understand. It seems so simple?" Cheryl asked. "We experience human resource problems every day that would not exist if people could understand the difference between purpose and objective."

"Cheryl, wars are fought over the meaning of words. It is simple to explain but it is not easy to defuse the anger. People have emotional scars from the battles and they hold grudges for years, sometimes centuries, over inaccurate definitions of terms. That's why we will examine emotional learning as a major part of the leadership challenge. We can't deal with it logically as you can see from Ron and Ariel. Neither will let go because the real problem between them didn't start with today's discussion. Their bags were packed long ago, right Ariel?"

"It's been going on between our departments for years. We wouldn't have all the customer service problems if his guys would stop promising customers what we can't deliver," Ariel said in protest.

Before Ron could say anything I quickly said, "We need to add another Learn To item to our list." I moved to the flip chart and added, *Learn to underpromise and overdeliver.* I looked at Ron and said, "Make sure you do this tomorrow, Ron. A 4 handicap might put you in an overpromised position."

Ron just looked at me. He didn't know how to respond, so I said, "Unless there are any more questions let's move on."

It was now 3:30 and the air was out of the balloon. The argument between Ron and Ariel had taken them back to the reality of their real world. The focus had switched to the helpless, hopeless state of arguments and blame. The whacking and blame game had returned, so I consciously decided to defer the discussion about competitive advantage.

"We are nearly done for today," I said. "I want to prepare you for what will happen tomorrow on the golf course. You will have a choice as to your level of participation. You will be asked to stay involved at all times. You can decide whether you want to learn the Swing to Balance process. Here's what that means."

"My son Bill will join us tomorrow. He is both a teaching and a playing professional. He was not with us today so he won't have any bias toward you in any way. He will meet you as a professional golf instructor and treat you as if you want to learn how to play the game of golf. You will really enjoy your experience with Bill."

"Could he beat Ron?" Ariel asked.

"I don't know. I haven't seen Ron play?" I didn't want to start the war again.

"We will start in this room at 8:00. You will be paired with a partner who will help you learn the Swing to Balance process. You will be a coach and be coached."

"Better add *Learn to coach and be coachable* to the Learn To list," Sharon suggested.

"I'll add it," volunteered Mark. "I want to see someone coach Ron."

I laughed and said, "Ron, it sounds like you'll have a heavy leadership burden tomorrow." Little did he know how true that was going to be? I continued, "The foursomes and pairings have already been established. We have tried to pair you with someone you don't work for and someone who needs your help."

"After a brief orientation, we will go to the driving range for approximately two hours. Your golf bag will be loaded on a cart with your partner's bag by the golf staff. I will ask that you obey our directions at all times. This is a major safety consideration. For example, you will not be allowed to hit balls for at least an hour. Please, I know the temptation, but it is very important for everyone's safety that you refrain. There will be plenty of time to hit balls."

"On the driving range, you will be helping your partner create muscle memory. This will require careful attention to holding the club is specific body positions. Imposing a discipline and focus while you are doing this is a very important leadership issue. When the safety of others is at stake, there can be no fooling around. We'll give you all the proper direction on the range. We've never had anyone get hurt, and I promise you we will have fun again tomorrow."

"The purpose of the Simulation is to extract business principles from the game of golf. To give you one example, golf is a game without conflict. It is totally a proactive game. If you recall, one of the seven habits is to *Be Proactive,*" I said.

"How is golf proactive?" Ariel asked.

"Good question. The ball just sits on the tee. The course doesn't attack you. The flag doesn't move around on the green. Everything is right there for you to see in advance. There are no surprises," I suggested.

"Until you hit it in the weeds," chided Ron.

"Stop it. You will be her partner tomorrow," I suggested. "You won't want her to hit it in the weeds then."

"Yes he will," said Sharon. "You don't know Ron." Everyone laughed except Ron.

"After the driving range, we will have a box lunch, relax for thirty minutes, then use our new Swing to Balance skills on the course. We will play only nine holes. And there will be real money for the winning group." I put a stack of 400 one-dollar bills on the table in front of me. I added, "And the prize money will triple if the group breaks par." I added another $800 to the pile.

"Wow! Look at all that money!" someone said. "You'll be rich, Ron," someone else yelled. Ron looked very confident.

"Break par! Are you kidding? We'll be lucky to break a hundred for nine," someone shouted.

"You will be amazed by your potential after you learn to Swing to Balance. The game may be different," I suggested.

"Is there a trick in this thing somewhere?" Jill asked.

"Some things may surprise you, but there are no tricks. It's a matter of how you interpret the rules, right Brad?" I said as I looked at Legal. He was not paying much attention. He had checked out long ago.

"Will I be embarrassed?" asked Kathy. "I don't even know how to hold a club."

"The potential exists for everyone to be embarrassed some time tomorrow. The purpose is not, however, to embarrass you. It is more accurate to say you will all be frustrated at times. That will be part of the emotional learning experience for everyone," I added. "But we have all been frustrated many times in our lives and we are generally richer because of those experiences."

"Any final questions?"

"Who gets to coach the Chairman?" someone asked.

"The Chairman will be Bob's partner," I replied.

This is Al. You've noticed that I was quiet after lunch. I didn't want my excitement to show or spoil the fun for anyone by pretending to know it all. Tom had told me how the Simulation experience would work, but I'm clueless as to what is actually going to happen on the course. I can't imagine what will be so challenging for us except to learn to Swing to Balance. My bet is that Ron will not even try it. He'll try to impress everyone with how good he already is.

I sure hope the Ariel and Ron show doesn't ignite again. It would be nice to rid the company of that feud. As for me, I'm going to sneak down to the driving range tonight and practice Swinging to Balance. I sure hope I don't swing and miss. That would be embarrassing. Here we go.

Chapter 13
Simulate the Future

Bill and I arrived at the course at 7:00 a.m. It was going to be a perfect day for golf. When it rains, people grumble and we tell them there are times the business environment isn't fun. Today there will be no excuses.

Bill had played in a one-day local tournament on Monday. As we shook hands I said, "Good morning. How'd you play yesterday?"

"Shot 68. Was third. Sixty-six won it," Bill said.

"Is this group ready?" he asked.

"This will be an amazing experience to watch. The orange ball will be traumatic," I said.

Bill laughed and asked, "Who's going to be the victim?"

"His name is Ron. He's the vice president of Sales. He's a 4 handicap and thinks he has the money won. He has no clue what's going to happen to him," I said.

Bill laughed and shook his head. We've seen the act of many guys like Ron. We began to unload the car and I said, "It could also be the Chairman. He's an avid golfer. Plays every day. It could be him. It will be fun to watch."

"The Chairman? Who's he?" Bill asked.

"I haven't met him. His name is Frank Shamanski. He wasn't here yesterday. The CEO invited him. He thinks he's coming to play golf. He apparently has played all over the world. Should be an interesting guy to watch."

"Does he know this is a business Simulation?" Bill asked.

"I'm not sure what the CEO told him. His expectations will change very quickly," I said.

Bill laughed, "The old meet or exceed customer expectations thing. How many times have we heard that?"

There wasn't time for much conversation. Bill went to the pro shop to begin the arrangements for the driving range. I went inside to pass out the coaching manuals. Each participant receives a three-ring binder that contains all the coaching materials and the Swing to Balance lesson plans.

As I walked into the room, Al was already there. "Good morning. Going to be a great day. What brings you out so early?" I asked.

"Thought you might need some help. I've been awake since 5:00. Couldn't drink any more coffee so I thought I'd come over and see if I could help in some way."

"Sure. You can put the coaching manuals around the tables."

I pointed to the boxes that contained the manuals. "You look great in your Swing to Balance shirt," I said.

We had given all the participants a Swing to Balance golf shirt before they left yesterday. The shirts look nice and subtly suggest that they are all a team. They don't think of it that way.

Within minutes Bob and the Chairman walked in. "Tom, I want you to meet Frank Shamanski our Chairman. Frank, this is Tom. He and his son Bill will be our teachers for today."

"Good morning Frank. I'm glad you could join us."

"Wouldn't miss a chance to play a round of golf," Frank said. "Bob has told me a little about what happened yesterday on the way over. Are you sure I won't be an intrusion?"

"Not at all. Actually we needed another player when Rene cancelled," I said, "But I must warn you, this is a business Simulation on the golf course not a round of golf on a business day. We will be using golf as a metaphor to learn about leadership and business."

"Sounds great. Wouldn't want it any other way. They need some leadership training," he said.

Why is it that the senior executives don't think they need training in leadership? I thought to myself.

"Anything we can do to help set up?" Bob asked.

"I'd suggest you introduce Frank to those who don't know him. That would be the most important thing. We can then get started without additional introductions."

As they walked away, I heard Frank ask Bob why Rene cancelled. I didn't hear the answer, but I saw a negative reaction from Frank.

Al said, "Did you hear that? *We* need leadership training. Like he doesn't."

"I heard it. That's very common thinking within his business model. Wait until 5:00. It might change," I suggested.

The rest of the group arrived and the excitement was buzzing about the money. I had stacked the $1,200 prize money on the table in front of the room. Everyone came up to touch it. There is something about real money that inspires the passion of people.

Ron walked over to the money, picked it up and said for everyone to hear, "This will be mine by the end of today." Everyone booed. The game was on.

Ariel looked at the money and asked me, "Is there any way I can win this?"

"You have as much chance as anyone. It has very little to do with your golf ability," I added.

She shouted at Ron as he walked away, "Did you hear that big shot. It's mine!"

I heard Tina mumble, "Here we go again."

"Good morning everyone. We need to get started. The prize money has already ignited your passion. In front of you is a coaching manual. Inside there is a nametag. Please put your first name on it so that Bill will know your name."

Bill walked in. "Let me introduce you to Bill. He will be your golf professional for today. He will teach you everything he knows about golf, if you ask. Welcome Bill."

Everyone gave Bill a round of applause. Then someone shouted, "Is everything your dad told us true? Did he really listen to you about the clubs?"

Bill laughed and joked, "It's all a lie. He can't break 80. Try him out today. Ask him to hit a shot for you if you want to find out. You'll be amazed," Bill came toward me and gave me a high five.

I said, "He's the pro. I have an excuse for bad shots." Bill and I laughed knowing what was in store for them on the course.

"If you will open the coaching manual to the Introduction section, we must get started," I said.

I began to read the Introduction. By the third paragraph I had their attention. It read, "It is important to realize that this is a Business Simulation on a golf course, not a round of golf on a business day. A Simulation is a real life experience designed to accelerate the potential to learn new concepts, principles, and perspectives. During the next seven hours you will learn something about the following items:

Learn to trust the total group to make intelligent decisions
Learn new leadership commands
Learn to tell the truth
Learn to influence effectively
Learn to learn
Learn to let go
Learn to make choices
Learn to treat people like people
Learn to listen
Learn to be patient
Learn to keep promises
Learn to bet wisely
Learn the rules of the game before playing
Learn to be humble
Learn to link priorities to vision
Learn to underpromise and overdeliver
Learn to coach and be coachable."

I had printed the Learn To list from the previous day and inserted it in their manuals. "The Simulation will require alignment, effective coaching, developing a strategy, taking action without knowing how, being coached, and a host of other items that you see on the list."

"Today's business environment has many paradoxical dilemmas. Yesterday, we talked about Mass Customization. To the Mass Production mind of most executives Mass and Customized are impossible. It is the same dilemma you face—standard products or specials." I paused to be certain everyone was listening. Ron was talking to Ariel and not listening.

The silence got his attention and I continued, "A paradox is two tension resolution points that must exist in a simultaneous state. Other paradoxical situation that you are familiar with are quantity and quality, empowerment and control, flexible and low cost, global and local."

When I said global and local, I looked toward the Chairman. He confidently nodded his head. From that gesture I could tell he was listening.

The Introduction went on to suggest, "Golf is a paradoxical game. It requires effortless-effectiveness. The more effortless the swing the straighter the shot. By the end of today you will also understand the meaning of frustrating-fun."

When we finished the Introduction, I asked them to turn to the second section where the process for the day was listed. We had inserted the pairings for the day in this section. "For the convenience of the golf staff and to maximize your learning experience, we have pre-assigned foursomes and playing partners."

Group 1	Ron and Ariel	Bryan and Brad
Group 2	Bob and Frank	Wally and Cheryl
Group 3	Al and Ralph	Jill and Kathy
Group 4	Tina and Mark	Sharon and Mike

There was a moment of silence as people searched for their name, and then there was a shrill scream from Ariel. "I have to play with Ron! No way!"

"Yes, Ariel you have the distinct privilege of being Ron's coach for the day."

"That's like being queen for a day?" someone yelled.

The nervous laughter in the room was buzzing. I looked at Ron and he was just sitting there expressionless. He said, "Does that mean I get to coach her too?"

"That's right Ron. Please be kind to Ariel," I added. "You may need her to win all that money."

Ron was too preoccupied plotting his defense to hear the comment I just made, but I could tell that a few others heard it.

We moved from the process section to the coaching section to review the following list:

Your Role As Coach

- Focus on the process of Swing to Balance
- Tell your partner what you see
- Facilitate muscle memory
- Be gentle: swinging a club is hard to do
- Be firm, don't let them quit trying
- Use pictures to help them visualize what they look like
- Ignore justification of incompetence
- Listen for speculation
- Neutralize blame with "It is" and "Not yet"
- Tell then what they did well; ignore what they did wrong
- Stay future focused, use 'try this next time'
- Acknowledge feeling, 'It is frustrating'
- Observe improvement
- Watch for fatigue
- Acknowledge Balance in the Swing
- Never say hit it.

Your Role As Partner

- Try the new game
- Commit to play the game
- Accept feedback without criticism
- Share how you are feeling
- Don't speculate or blame.

I briefly explained the coaching process and showed them how the coaching manual was set up to help them. I told them we would show them how to use the manual once we were on the range.

"Question?" I could see several hands in the air. Ariel asked, "Do you mean I have to coach Ron and I don't know anything about golf?"

"That's right. You will be a great coach for him. He'll learn a lot from you, Ariel," I added. Little did she know at this point how true that would be. The learning would not be anything about golf, but she thought it meant golf.

"We need to get started. Turn to Section 9. There you will find the rules and the prize money. As you can see, there is a lot of money at stake today. There is a $400 prize for the winning group. And if that group breaks par in the process, the prize money will be $1,200." I waved the money high in the air. Some people were excited. Some were immediately defeated, knowing that they did not know how to play golf and the likelihood of them winning was zero.

"Why don't you just give it to Ron right now," Brad the lawyer suggested. "No one can beat him."

"I wouldn't be so sure about that," suggested the Chairman. "It says we are going to play by USGA Rules and I'm sure Ron will have difficulty with that format," he said. "He will likely get disqualified before the round is over," he laughed.

I looked toward Ron and he was unable to talk. That statement implied that he would cheat sometime during the round. Now I know what Bob meant by intimidation.

"If there are any questions about the rules, we'll let Brad be the judge. Okay Brad?" I laughed. "USGA Rules are very precise and well defined. Brad can interpret them for you. If Brad is not around, Bill knows all the rules. He can help you." Bill nodded his head and smiled. Little did they realize how the rules would affect the outcome of the day.

Everyone started to get up and Bob shouted, "Wait, I want to say something."

Everyone stood silently as Bob said in a very traditional way, "I want you to have fun today. Like anything we do in the training arena, you'll only get out of this what you put into it. I am excited to have Frank join us. We're going to give it our all. Let's go have a blast."

It was fun to watch the participants leave for the range. The expectations varied from Ron, who had been on a practice range a 1000 times before, to Ariel, who had never been on a driving range in her life.

This is Al. I can't tell you how excited I was. The only problem I had was that I was paired with Ralph. He at least had golf shoes on. I knew he didn't play golf on a regular basis, but the clubs in his bag were Titleist. The reality was settling in. The time had arrived. You know the feeling. You have to take the field. For those who had played golf before, the drive out to the range was a nonevent. For those who had never been there before, I could sense the anxiety. None of us were thinking about business. It seemed to be all about golf.

As I drove to the range, I started to think of how what we were doing connects from a business perspective, but my mind quickly went back to golf as the range came into view. I relaxed and decided to let what happens, happen. We were soon to find out. Tag along. You'll enjoy the experience.

Chapter 14
How You Practice Really Matters

"Welcome to Swing to Balance. What you are about to experience is a business Simulation conducted on the golf course. It starts right now. There is a space in your notebook to record any observations you might make from a business perspective. We will not process what you observe until after the golf course experience."

"Does that mean we should be paranoid about what's happening to us?" asked Wally.

"Do some people appear paranoid at work every day?" I asked.

"Sure," he responded.

"Then make a note to yourself that you felt paranoid at the beginning. That's what the note section is for. Record you feelings, suspicions, and observations at any time. After golf, you will have a story to read that might reveal something very interesting. On the other hand, you don't have to record anything. Just relax and enjoy the Simulation. We will extract the meaning tomorrow," I said.

"I'd rather do it that way," Ariel said. "I have Ron to deal with. That will be plenty."

Everyone laughed and Wally reached for his notebook and started writing.

"What did I say that was newsworthy, Wally?" Ariel demanded.

"You'll find out later," he said.

"Bill, take over."

"Hi everyone. I'm Bill and as you were told, I'll be your golf professional for the rest of the day. If I were you, I would be asking myself the question, can he hit the ball? Or said in the correct way, can he Swing to Balance? So, let me quickly demonstrate the Swing to Balance golf swing before we begin to teach it to you."

Bill teed up a ball, set-up, and swung the club. *Crack*—long and straight.

"Wow!" was the universal response from the group.

"One more just to be sure the first one wasn't a fluke."—*Crack*—same result.

I could see Wally writing in his book. I'm confident that Wally will be our annotator for the day.

Bill spent the next five minutes giving them more information about his background. He quickly told the story how he had helped me with my swing when he returned from golf school. Everyone laughed when Bill suggested that I still need his help. They didn't realize that every golfer has a coach and that coaching never stops.

"Let's begin to learn the Balanced golf swing. We will demonstrate the process to you as a total group, then ask you to spread out over the range and work with your partner on the specific lessons. Please, do not try to hit balls until we tell you," Bill said.

The balls were in baskets but not available to them. Someone always tries to hit a ball unless we are emphatic about the safety aspects of the process.

"The Swing to Balance method of learning golf starts at the end of a perfect swing and works backward. If you play golf and your current swing is not correct, you must replace the muscle memory of your old swing with what is correct. If you already swing correctly, the Balanced Finish position will not feel strange. If you have never played golf, you will be programming your muscle memory correctly from the beginning."

Bill motioned to me to assume the Balance Finish position. "This is called Balanced Finish. In this position the body is tall. The left leg is straight. The right shoulder is well past the left. The head is up, looking at the target. The belt buckle is pointing to the target. The right toe is straight up. If the right shoe was a nail, you could drive it into the ground. Your weight is totally on the left leg. Pick up your right toe and tap it. The hands are beside your left ear and the club is behind your back."

Head up looking at target

Belt Buckle pointing at target

Left leg is straight

Body is tall

Center of Gravity

Right Shoulder past left

Right foot pointed up

Weight on left foot

Axis of rotation

Bottom of shoe completely visible

Balanced Finish

Bill held my body in the Balanced Finish position and touched every part of my body as he was describing the process. "The key is to *feel* your body in this position so you can repeat it over and over again. This is called muscle memory programming. If your body doesn't know where it must go, it won't get there."

I could see Wally reaching for his notebook, and excitedly he said, "That's start with the end in mind, everybody!"

Bill said, "You're right, Wally. You must start with the end of the swing in your muscle memory. If you don't know the end of the swing, you will stop somewhere short of Balanced Finish after the club hits the ball."

Cynically, Ron asked, "How do we know this is right? We saw you hit a ball, but why does the swing always have to end in Balance?"

Bill walked to his golf cart parked beside the range and lifted a large four-inch binder and said, "In this binder are the pictures of many famous professionals including Tiger Woods, David Duval, Annika Sorenstam, Kerri Webb, and many others. There are pictures of at least forty different golfers, and their swings all end in Balanced Finish. If anyone at any time doubts the Swing to Balance process, we will be glad to show you the same position in the pros." He opened the binder and said, "Here is a picture of Tiger Woods when he was three years old. Notice the position is he in?"

The picture showed Tiger in Balanced Finish at the age of three.

"Too bad your dad didn't teach you this when you were three, Ron," said Tina.

Bill continued, "It is okay to question the source of the teaching. You must always challenge the source of any consultant's material and advice. Many companies have been steered wrong by the latest management fad." Bill looked at Wally and said, "Got that Wally?"

Sharon said, "I'm going to trust that Wally will get all the business points." Everyone laughed as Wally was writing in his book.

"Taking notes will be more fun for me than learning the swing," Wally added.

Bill quickly added, "Maybe you should do both."

"If you turn to Section 4 in your coaching manual, you will see the Balanced Finish lesson described in detail. In a moment I'll want you to spread out across the range and begin to help your partner with this first lesson. One word of caution! When you are working with your partner, always secure the club in this fashion while standing behind them." Bill demonstrated what he meant and showed them how they could be hit it the face by the club if they were not careful. "Also stretch your partners muscles slowly. Your partner may not have the flexibility to assume this position at first. In other words, be careful and go slow," he encouraged.

The participants were anxious to begin. As the individual lessons began, everyone quickly realized that what looks simple is not easy.

"It looks so easy when you and Bill did it," Tina said. She was working with Mark and having difficulty getting Mark to balance on his left leg.

"It is not easy. It's like riding a bike. You'll fall off many times before you learn to balance. Fortunately, in this case you won't get hurt." I laughed as Mark fell backward when Tina pushed him up to the Balanced Finish position. "Go slow and keep trying," I said.

I could see Bill at the end of the range working with Bob and Frank. They were both trying to learn the process. That was a relief for me. I was concerned that Frank might resist.

I walked toward Ron and Ariel and Ariel remarked, "I never thought I would let him put his hands on me. Now he's going to touch me all day long. I'm not sure I can stand it," she joked.

Ron was helping Ariel with the Balanced Finish position. "Hold the club Ron." I warned, "She'll hit you in the chops."

"I know. She almost did." They were having fun starting out, at least while Ron was coaching Ariel.

"Why don't you switch and let Ariel help you," I suggested. Ron picked up his club, assumed the Balanced Finish position and said, "How's that?" directing the question to me. He could hold it without any help from Ariel.

"What do you think, Ariel?" I asked. She wasn't sure. Bill had just arrived from helping the Chairman, so I suggested she ask Bill what he thought.

Bill showed Ariel how to use the coaching manual to diagnose Ron's position. "It looks goods except he's still standing a little on his right foot. Help him get his right toe up so he can pick it up and tap it." Bill showed Ariel how to reposition Ron's right foot.

Ron immediately lost his balance. "I don't swing that far," he remarked. "If I go that far, I'd hook the ball."

"That's probably true." Bill said and he walked on to help others.

After ten minutes we reconvened the total group for the next lesson, the Balanced Set-up.

"The next position is the Balanced Set-up shown in Section 5 of your manual," Bill announced.

"Are all the steps as hard as that first one?" someone asked. "I haven't mastered the Balanced Finish yet."

"You will repeat the Balanced Finish position many times as we proceed through all the positions. It is a part of every lesson," Bill encouraged. "It takes time to develop Balance. Did you get that Wally?" Bill laughed as he saw Wally writing feverishly.

Al blurted out, "Trust me, it just happens once you get it all together."

"We'll never trust you again, Al," someone yelled. They were having fun with Al's serious admonishment.

Bill began by saying, "The Balanced Set-up is also a difficult position for some people to achieve. It puts a strain on the lower back, so go slow." Bill reached for a club and demonstrated the set-up process. "Put the club across your body where your legs join your hip joints. It's right below the belt line for most people. Now, lock your knees back and stand tall from the waist up. Then, using the club push your rear end back and up and simultaneously lean your chest and head out over your toes. Make sure to keep your back straight. You will feel your weight move to your heels and your toes will start to come off the ground." Bill demonstrated the process several times.

He continued, "Once you are in this position, unlock your knees without letting your rear end come under you. Your weight should now be on the middle of your feet. Now, drop your arms. Shake them. See how relaxed they are, and now grip the club."

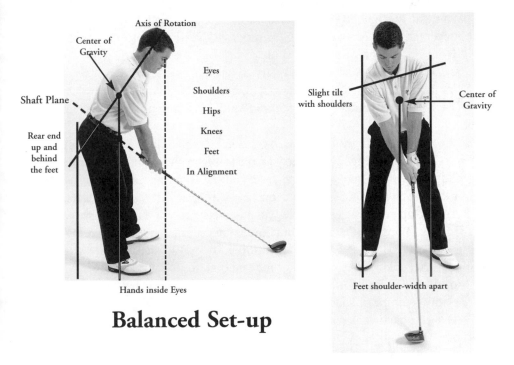

Balanced Set-up

Bill did it again, then asked me to demonstrate the process while he pointed to the various steps. Once I was in Balanced Set-up Bill said, "In the Balanced Set-up position you could now play quarterback in football, shortstop in baseball, wrestle, or defend in basketball. This is a universal athletic position."

"The most common mistake in the Balanced Set-up process is to let the rear end come back under the body and to round the back," Bill said as he demonstrated those two most common mistakes.

"You mean the butt?" Chided Brad the lawyer. "Why don't you call it what it is?" he added.

Bill had not heard the accuracy of definition argument from yesterday. Bill politely said, "It is the butt, but I refer to it as the rear end. It is difficult for me to tell people at the driving range to get their butt up. That's embarrassing for some people." Everyone laughed and Wally started taking notes again.

Someone yelled, "That's not the end we have in mind, Wally."

Bill chuckled and continued the lesson by showing them the proper way to connect the Balanced Set-up position to Balanced Finish. He demonstrated the process several times. "Spread out on the range now and start to link these two static positions together into a dynamic swing. Do not take a backswing," Bill said.

"That's linking priorities to vision!" Wally yelled with excitement.

Bill looked at Wally and smiled. "You're amazing," Bill said. "That is exactly right."

As the participants began to work with their partners, I noticed that Wally was so busy writing he was ignoring his responsibility to coach Cheryl. I went over to help her and noticed that she was not enjoying the process. "Need some help?" I asked

"No. I'll wait for Wally," she said.

"I can't wait to hear the story Wally is writing," I suggested.

"Yeah, it will be precise as always," Cheryl cynically added.

The Chairman came over to me and said, " Your son is impressive. This is great."

I excused myself from Cheryl by saying, "Make sure Wally practices the Swing to Balance swing. He'll need to perform on the course." I turned to the Chairman and said, "Thank you. I'm glad you are enjoying yourself."

Bill was over working with Ron and Ariel. Ron was demonstrating the Balanced Set-up process to Ariel. He was just doing it, which was very natural for him. He was skipping the lock your knees step, and Ariel was having trouble getting into the Balanced Set-up position. After Bill showed her the proper sequence Ariel said, "That's easy. Let me see you do it, Ron."

Ariel handed Ron the club and he did it his old way. "That's easy. That's the way I always set-up," he added.

"But you have your rear-end under you. If I look at this picture and compare it to your body right now, your back is a little round. Isn't that right?" Ariel said looking at Bill for confirmation.

"She's right, Ron. You have a slight rear-end under set-up. It isn't bad, but that's why you are still standing on your right foot at Finish. Try to Swing to Balance from your normal set-up and you'll see what I mean," Bill suggested.

Ron swung up to Balance and sure enough was still standing on his right foot at Finish. "You mean I have to go all the way to here?" and he stood up straight and tall.

"That's what the picture shows," Ariel said.

"You're getting it," Bill said with some encouragement to Ariel.

"Getting what?" she asked.

"The coaching thing. You're learning that you don't have to be able to play golf to coach. All you need is a picture of perfect and you can translate that picture into the physiology of another person's body. That's why you can be Ron's coach today. Amazing isn't it?" and Bill began to walk away.

"Wait." Bill turned and Ariel said, "That's the vision thing isn't it? Without the picture of perfect we couldn't do this. Right?"

"You are very observant." Bill continued on to help Bob and the Chairman.

I smiled inside and thought, *Good move to pair Ron and Ariel together. Maybe they'll get over their anger toward each other at work.*

We used the same process to teach everyone the next lesson called the Toll Booth. Bill continued the lessons by saying, "The next position is called the Toll Booth and before someone asks what that means, let me explain. The backswing is a very difficult move. There are many mistakes that can be made in swinging the club back from the Balanced Set-up position, so we developed a visual aid called the Toll Booth. If you are driving down a toll road and come to the toll booth, you must slow down, throw money in the basket and then move forward. Can everyone picture that narrow slot on the toll road?" Bill asked.

"I want you to visualize that narrow slot right here." Bill held his hands in position and asked me to demonstrate the turn to the Toll Booth position. I set-up and turned the club to Bill's waiting hands. "In this position you will notice that the club is a natural extension of the left arm, the handle of the club is pointing straight down the target line, and the toe of the club is pointing straight up. It is also important to maintain your spine angle," Bill said.

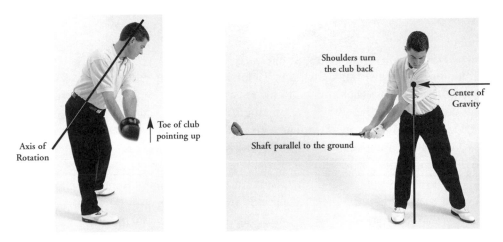

Toll Booth

It is at this point in the Swing to Balance lessons that the beginners begin to get overwhelmed. Bill finished the explanation of the Toll Booth lesson quickly by saying, "We're almost ready to swing at some balls. Work with your partner and swing from the Toll Booth to Balanced Finish. The swing should now start to feel complete."

Once again the practice regime was similar. Ron was demonstrating the process rather than helping Ariel. Wally and Cheryl had nearly quit. Frank and Bob were doing very well, and Al and Ralph seemed to be storming at each other.

After the Top of the Backswing lesson, Bill announced, "It's time to swing at some balls." A loud cheer went up and the dash was on for the buckets of balls over on the side of the range.

Axis of Rotation

Balanced triangle with club in the middle

Braced right knee

Shoulders turned 90º

Center gravity over right foot

Hips turned 45º

Top of Back Swing

"Before you begin swing at the balls, let me give you the proper coaching command. You must think Swing to Balance. When the ball appears, your brain and right hand have been trained to hit at the ball." Bill demonstrated what might happen. "You must believe that, you swing the club to Balance, the club hits the ball. Let me show you by swinging with my eyes closed."

Bill swung with his eyes closed and—*Crack*—long and straight. "Ready? Begin swinging."

Bill and I stood back and watched and the first thing we heard was "Wow! Look at that!" The results are instantaneous for some people. "This is amazing!" Others were struggling. "You're hitting at it—Swing to Balance." The coaching was going well.

I pointed to Ron and Ariel and said, "Watch this."

Ariel was struggling to get the ball airborne. She tried three times and Ron said, "Let me show you." Ron launched one into the air. He hits it a long way with a little draw.

"Nice shot, Ron." Bill said. Ron puffed his chest and hit another under the watchful eye of Bill.

"Bet that draw turns into a nasty hook when you play bad," Bill commented.

"Either that or I block it right," Ron said

Ariel asked, "What's a hook and a block? That's Greek to me."

"This is a hook."—Ron launched a high shot curving right to left. "And this is a block." He hit one high and to the right.

Bill said, "You are very talented. You can do that on command. Can you control it on the course?" he asked.

"Both shots show up when I don't want them at times. That's what keeps me a 4 handicap. I always have one or two doubles a round," Ron said.

"What's a double?" Ariel asked.

"You aren't going to ask all these questions all day are you?" Ron asked in jest.

"Sure. Remember that this is about business. I may find something out that I will need for tomorrow," she said.

"She's right, Ron," I added. "You may have to explain a lot of things to her before it's over."

Ron took my statement to mean that he had to show Ariel how to play golf, not help her learn how to play. The rest of the range time was spent with Ariel watching Ron hit shots. He showed her how to chip and told her why the ball went left or right depending on the path of the club at impact. Bill and I just chuckled to ourselves thinking, *If he only knew what was going to happen.*

It was obvious that Wally and Cheryl were going to have a difficult time on the course. Cheryl was a decent player and was not helping Wally with his swing. Wally was practicing alone when Bob yelled from across the range, "Swing to Balance, Wally." That drew attention to Wally and he stopped swinging and began to write something in his manual. Bob yelled again, "Whatcha writing, Wally?"

Cheryl yelled back, "He's convinced he has this thing figured out. You know, he's paranoid." Cheryl meant it jokingly but I could tell the paranoid comment was not going down well with Wally.

The ball baskets were nearly empty when we called an end to the practice session. Some people were already exhausted. For those who have never played golf before, the range experience is almost enough for one day.

I announced "The box lunches are back at the Club House on the table outside the pro shop. Relax for a half-hour. We'll be ready to tee off and take your game to the course at noon."

The Chairman approached me as we were picking up some paper from the range and said, "That was the best lesson I ever had. Where did you guys learn this?"

"That's a long story. Let's just say it's in all the golf magazines and on the Golf Channel. It's a matter of how you see it and how it's taught. Bob can tell you the story I told the group yesterday," I suggested.

This is Al. At this point, I'm excited but Ralph's a drag. He's fighting the coaching process. He thinks I'm being critical, just like at work. Either I need to learn to coach differently or he needs to learn to be coachable. Probably a little of both. Anyway we aren't talking to each other as we drive back to get lunch. Maybe that's our problem at work. We're both a little stubborn and withdraw to our own worlds. I'll ask Tom for some advice before we go out to play.

The rest of the group, except for Wally, is doing well. The nongolfers did great. They weren't hitting 300-yard drives, but they were hitting them straight. Tom is right, if you swing the club to Balance and miss hit the ball, it will still go straight.

Everyone forgot about the money, but I think Ron's group will probably win. He is good. We all watched him launch that new 45-inch driver he has. He hits it farther than Bill. Not always straight, but man can he hit it a long way.

I was amazed how the Chairman responded to the lessons. I thought a player of his experience would resist learning a new way to swing. He said the Club championships were coming up and he hoped that taking a lesson wouldn't screw up his swing. He tried all the things Bill showed him. I'm glad he's not intimidating anyone.

I hope we play a scramble. It will be miserable watching all the beginners get around the course. They'll never finish. Some of them are already tired.

Stay tuned. It gets exciting from here on. The best is yet to come.

Chapter 15
The Orange Ball

Wally approached me when I arrived at the Club House and said, "I think I have this thing figured out. It's a total group game, isn't it?" Even after all the ribbing on the range, he seemed excited.

"What makes you think that?" I asked.

"We all have the same shirts on and the first Learn To is to make effective decisions as a total group. Bill explained each lesson to us as a total group. And based on the discussion about the meaning of words from yesterday, I'm thinking that total group means all of us. Am I right?"

"That's certainly one way to see it," I said "Have you suggested that to any of the others?" I asked.

"No. I'm not going to tell anyone. They won't listen to me. You heard them. They think I'm paranoid," he laughed.

His laugh made me feel better. There are some people who can't take the ribbing and I was concerned about the treatment Wally got on the range.

"Why do they accuse you of being paranoid?" I asked.

"I'm always reading things into stuff that they don't think matters. You know? That's the way software engineers are. They always accuse my group of being weird," Wally explained.

"Who's *they?*" I asked.

"You know. Everyone," he said.

The amorphous they is getting him. I thought to myself. *Why is there always a conspiracy in people's minds that some fictitious they or them are out to get them?*

"I think I know, but maybe you should try telling everyone again," I suggested.

"I'd rather put a Learn To on the list and if I'm right, they would need to learn to listen to me tomorrow," he offered.

"We already have Learn to listen on the Learn To list. Does that cover it?" I asked

"Yeah, I guess it does. But I'm not going to tell anyone what I'm thinking right now. I could be wrong," Wally added.

"That's your choice," I said. "How did the Swing to Balance swing work for you?" I asked.

"It didn't work very well, but Cheryl can do it," he said.

I had to go to the first tee and finish arrangements with the starter. "Well, good luck on the course. We'll see if your hunch is right." I walked away.

I thought to myself, *I understand why some people think he's paranoid. Then I thought, Why are people who have ideas unable or unwilling to share them? Why do they fear being wrong? Why doesn't the organization listen to people like Wally?*

When I arrived at the first tee, Bill was looking for me. He said, "The starter said we could go as soon as we're ready."

"Do we have the orange balls?" I asked. Bill handed me the shag-bag of balls and four brand new carefully marked orange balls.

"Do you know who the orange ball players will be?" he laughed.

"Have them tagged," I said.

I told Bill what Wally had told me. "Do you think he'll tell them?" he asked.

"He might, but I doubt whether they'll listen to him," I said. "You know the drill?"

"It wouldn't matter to Ron," Bill said. "He thinks he has the money in his pocket."

"You sure have him figured out," I said

"Didn't take long. Are you going to give Ariel the orange ball?" Bill laughed.

"Of course. That's why we're here."

Bill went to do a final check to be certain that the head pro had not scheduled any groups behind us for at least an hour. By now most of the players were on the putting green. I announced to the group that we were nearly ready to start and asked, "Does anyone need any golf balls?" I held up the shag-bag and everyone came running. Many of the nongolfers did not have any balls.

"There are plenty of balls. Help yourself. If you run out, we will have plenty available on the course at any time." I put the shag-bag down. It contained almost 500 balls and there was a feeding frenzy to swoop them up.

Ron did not take any and made sure I knew that he had enough balls and that he played only balata Titleist, 100 Compression. "Those are good balls," I said, and I walked away.

I mingled with the players as they were getting balls and casually handed one of the new orange balls to Tina and said, "Here's an orange one. It might bring you good luck."

"That is a nice one. Didn't know they came in colors," she said.

"There are some yellow ones in the shag-bag unless they're all gone," I suggested.

I gave an orange ball in similar fashion to Ralph, Ariel, and Wally. The inconspicuous manner in which it was done did not seem significant to them, and none of their playing partners knew that they had the orange ball. Little did they know the significance of the orange ball.

I carefully watched Wally as he moved toward his golf bag and notebook. As with everything else, he seemed to attach some significance to the orange ball. He looked at it and made a notation in his manual. I laughed to myself and thought, *Maybe he is paranoid?*

"We're ready to go," I announced. "What are the rules?" someone asked. "How can we win the money?" was another question.

I gathered the total group and went over the rules section in their coaching manual. I turned to Section 9 and read, "USGA Rules apply. The scoring system will be best ball of your group. Record the one best score on your score card after each hole. As it says in Section 9, the group with the lowest score will win $400. It also says, if your group breaks par, the prize money will triple. That's $1,200, so Swing to Balance."

"Fat chance of breaking par. I don't even remember how to Swing to Balance," I heard from the crowd. "What does USGA stand for?" was another question.

Bill and I smiled at each other as the moment of truth arrived. They are about to play a game that many of them have never played before, and they don't even know the language of the new game. *Just like yesterday. No one knew the rules of Mass Customization then, and very few know USGA Rules now. Oh well, that's why they're here* I thought.

"Let me have your attention one more time," I shouted. "To assist the beginners, you can all borrow a shot from Bill at any time during the round. Only one shot per person. Bill will be roving the course and will be glad to assist you with a shot if it will help your score."

Bill said, "It might be wise to use me on the tough shots over water or on the par 3s." He was giving them a clue, but it did not register at this time. Later, it would become very obvious to them how Bill's assistance could help.

"Only one shot all day?" someone asked.

"Only one per person," I answered.

"I was going to have him play the entire round for me," someone joked.

Ron's group was first and he chose to go last. Ariel said, "I'm not going first, there's water right there."

Brad, the attorney decided to go first and hit a nice drive across the water. The tension was relieved. "At least we have one in play," Bryan remarked.

Bryan went next, and hit his ball in the water. Everyone groaned. "Swing to Balance, Bryan," came the command from the gallery. "That's easier said than done," he said as he teed up a second ball. His next shot went over the water and into the rough to the right.

It was now Ariel's turn. "You go next, Ron," she said in a very nervous way.

"Coach her Ron," I suggested. "It's her turn."

"Remember, start with the end in mind, Ariel," someone yelled. "Be positive. See the fairway on the other side," another person yelled, "You can do it, Ariel." The coaching came from all directions.

I looked at the group and said, "That's all good advice, but the best command is Swing to Balance, Ariel. Remember, coach the process," I suggested.

Ron said, "You can do it, just Swing to Balance." As Ariel put the tee in the ground, I could see that she was using the orange ball I had given her. I looked at Bill and he smiled and shrugged his shoulders. Ron said, "Take two practice swings then hit the ball—I mean Swing to Balance."

The silence was deafening. Ariel took two practice swings, approached the ball and hit the orange ball straight into the water. "Why did we have to start where there's water?" she yelled.

"That's the way the market is sometimes. It isn't always fair," I suggested. "Try again."

Ron confidently announced, "It's best ball, so you don't have to hit again. I'm going to make a par from here."

They were playing the down tees and the green was only 320 yards from there. "I can drive the green from here. We won't need your score. Let me go and you can hit again on the next tee," he added.

Ariel, relieved, backed away as Ron stepped forward, and with no practice swing nearly drove the green. "It's probably in that bunker next to the green," he said and walked confidently off toward the cart. "Come on. I'll carry the load on this hole," he said as they drove off toward the fairway.

Bill and I watched from the tee as they approached Brad's ball. Ron motioned for him to pick up, but Brad must have told him he wanted to play. Both Brad and Bryan hit their next shots toward the green. Neither shot made the putting surface.

I told the remaining groups that Bill would help them get started, and I drove off toward the first green. Ron was in the bunker ready to play his second shot before Brad and Bryan got to the green. As I approached in my cart, Ariel was standing outside the bunker with a rake. She joked, "I'm good for something. I'm the raker."

Ron hit a nice bunker shot to within 10 feet of the pin. Brad and Bryan were still trying to chip on and Ron told them to pick up, that he was going to make par. He almost made the putt for birdie, and he tapped it in for an easy par.

As the group headed toward the second tee, Bryan looked at me and said, "Sure glad we have a good player in our group."

As they arrived on the second tee, I said, "We have an email from the Chairman. I have printed copies and it reads, "The rules of the game have changed. See the attached. Good luck. Signed Frank." I handed them the new rules showing three new playing formats for the next seven holes. The new formats for playing were:

Format choices*	Hole numbers	Scoring
Everyone plays	Hole 1	Best ball of the group
Everyone plays	Holes 2–8	Total score of all players divided by 5 Maximum score per player = 12 Example: $$\frac{4+6+10+10}{5} = 6$$
Scramble	Holes 2–8	Gross score plus 2
Alternate shot	Holes 2–8	Gross score minus 1

*   You must use each format at least two times in the next seven holes. Note on your score card which format was used. Failure to use each format in this way is cause for disqualification.

There was silence as they studied the new rules. Ron quickly figured it out and said with disgust, "Great. There goes my round."

"I don't understand. What's a scramble?" Ariel asked.

They all gathered together and Ron tried to explain the different formats to them. Brad then noticed the new scoring formula and said, "If this is right, we could make a one on a par 3 with the alternate shot format. It says total score minus one. If we make a birdie, minus one, that's a one. Right?"

Ron looked at the scoring formula and said. "Yeah, we could make eagles with birdies on the par 4's and 5's too, but everyone has to hit good shots to do that," he said in a disgruntled way.

"Don't look at me that way," Ariel asserted.

"What way?" Ron said.

"You looked at me like I'm only a raker. I've only hit one shot so far and that went in the water. You mean I have to hit good shots? No way," she said.

The battle was started again, I thought to myself.

"We need to get going. The next group is almost finished on one. What format are we going to use here?" Bryan asked.

"It's a par 5, let's scramble," Ron said. "Everyone hit and we'll play from the best ball. From this tee, I can get home in two," he confidently added

Once again Ariel failed to get the ball airborne, and Ron told her, "Don't worry, I have you covered." As they drove off, I thought to myself, *What a hero. Wait until the ninth hole. His heroic approach will be useless.*

I remained behind to explain the rule change to the next group. It included Bob, the Chairman, Wally, and Cheryl. "What did you make on one?" I asked

"We made a double bogie," Bob answered. "Except for Wally, we all got across the water, but we all three-putted. These greens are really fast," he said.

I wondered whether Wally had lost the orange ball, but I didn't ask. He had a white one in his hand.

"Little trouble, Wally?" I asked.

"I'm not very good at this game. Good thing we have a couple of good players in our group," he said.

"Every group has some experienced players. It should be very fair," I added.

I proceeded to announce the rule change. The Chairman joked, "I don't remember sending that email."

Bob joked, "You were probably out of town and delegated it to me and I delegated it to Corporate Communications. You know how we communicate important stuff."

Everyone laughed and began to study the new rules. Like the first group, the alternate shot format was very appealing. "We subtract one on the alternate shot and have to add two on the scrambles," the Chairman observed. He thought a moment and said, "Let's just use the alternate shot format from here on."

"Can't do that," Bob said. "Says right here we must use all three formats at least two times in the next seven holes."

The Chairman thought again and said, "What about the ninth hole?"

"What do you mean?" asked Bob.

"Well, we've played one—seven more makes eight—that leaves the ninth hole unaccounted for," he said.

"Is this a misprint? Should it say *next eight holes?*" Bob looked at me and asked.

"The directions are correct," I said. "You sent them, Frank. Don't you remember?" I joked.

"It's a trick," Wally said. "I'll bet there will be another rule change on the ninth hole."

"There you go again, Wally, reading things into things," Bob said.

"There are no tricks," I said, "But Wally might be right" I laughed and said, "You better get going or I'll have to penalize you for slow play."

I drove back toward the first green where Al's group was just finishing. I looked back at the second tee as the Chairman teed off and they all headed toward the carts. They must have selected the alternate shot format. Wally was writing in his manual as Cheryl got in the driver side of the cart and slammed her foot on the accelerator pedal.

With Bill's help, the last group was now off the first tee and I could see Bill driving down the cart path toward me. He stopped and was laughing. "Two of the orange balls went in the water. Amazing to watch," he said

"Who lost them?" I asked.

"Ariel and Ralph hit them in the water. Tina and Wally played white balls. They must still have the orange ones," he said

"I'll catch up with Ron's group and see if they need a shot yet," Bill said. "I'll be interested to see if Ron borrows one from me," he added.

"I doubt it, but Ariel will need your help. Ron is ignoring her. She's become the raker. Encourage her to participate every chance you get," I said.

"I will," Bill said as he drove off to find them.

I drove back to the second tee and explained the new rules to Al's group. They were equally confused by the new scoring formats. Ralph was the orange ball player and seemed frustrated by the whole thing. I could tell he wasn't enjoying the experience.

"Make it over the water on the first hole, Ralph?" I asked.

"Are you kidding! Hit three in. Good thing you have lots of balls. We're going to need them. That money's pretty safe. No way we can beat Ron," he protested.

"You have Al in your group. He can Swing to Balance," I remarked.

"That doesn't matter. He can't putt. He three-putted the first green. We made a double bogey. Probably already two down." Ralph was mad.

"Well, don't quit," I said. "There's a lot of golf left. If you study the new rules carefully, you can make up ground fast. Don't forget you can each borrow a shot from Bill. If you do that in a strategic way, you will be amazed what can happen."

I drove back to the first green to see how Tina's group was doing. She was excited. "I hit the first one in the water, but got the second one over. I'm going to use that pretty orange ball you gave me on this hole. Maybe it will bring me good luck," she said.

"Hey, you got any more of those orange ones?" Sharon asked.

"That's all of the orange ones we had. There are some yellow ones here." I threw her a yellow ball from the shag-bag.

Tina said, "This Swing to Balance thing really works. It is amazing. It is just like my dad taught me when I was in high school. It's all coming back."

On the second tee the new rules were once again confusing to Tina's group. They also asked about the ninth hole.

Mike said, "You know the Chairman. He'll probably change his mind again before that. Let's not worry about the ninth. We have to play them one at a time."

"Good strategy," I suggested. "Remember you can each borrow a shot from Bill."

I was about to drive off when Tina asked, "Could I have asked Bill to hit my first tee shot?"

"Sure," I said

"I get it," she said.

"Get what?" asked Sharon.

"I'll tell you later. This is about business. We need to use the consultant at a very strategic time. Right?" she asked, looking at me for confirmation.

"Could be," I said. "Have fun."

This is Al. I double bogeyed the first hole as you heard. I didn't even hit it in the water. I missed the green. Hit it in the bunker. Blasted out and three-putted. When you think about golf, Swing to Balance is important, but it's the short game that really matters. I guess you don't worry about the short game if you don't have a long game. I don't know, but right now I want to quit. Glad I wasn't playing with the Chairman. I was a little cocky on the range. Guess I'll need to learn to be humble.

Ralph isn't adding to the fun. He's really a pain. He isn't even willing to try the Swing to Balance swing. He's just hitting it any way he can. Talk about commitment. I can see why we're having trouble at work. His attitude about doing something different is awful.

We've heard some laughing from Tina's group. Sounds like they're having fun. Bob and Frank must be doing well. They were gone from the second tee before we reached the first green. I feel very alone all of a sudden. I wrote that down in my manual under business thoughts. If you feel abandon and alone, it is hard to be motivated.

I have to find a way to relate with Ralph today. If it keeps going this way, he'll be negative about the whole experience tomorrow. I need to learn to coach someone who is negative. It would be easy right now to ignore him. I have a feeling that is not what I should do. Stay tuned. It gets exciting.

Chapter 16
Stop the Old Game

Hi. This is Bill. I'm going to take over from dad for the next three chapters and tell you how I see the Simulation from a golf professional perspective. I've taught hundreds of people the Swing to Balance method of swinging a golf club. It is truly amazing to watch beginners and advanced players make immediate changes in their golf ability.

From my perspective, I have learned that my brain can only focus on one swing thought at any moment. If I start a tournament with more than one swing thought for the day, I'm defeated before I start. When you see the players on TV worrying about their swing during the tournament, they struggle to compete. Vijay Singh's son was correct in telling his dad, *Trust your Swing, daddy*. That is why Swing to Balance is such a great command. It is not only simple; it is the most important command in golf.

The people in the golf Simulation have a very difficult time after the first hole. The same is true in business after any company announces a strategic change in direction. After the first hole, the participant must think within three separate and distinctly different contexts. Context is dad's term and an accurate one. I prefer the word focus. As a player, if I am focused on my swing, I am not focused on playing the course. The key to a golf professional's success is focus. It is very difficult to stay focused for eighteen holes. If I lose my focus, I make bogies.

When the scoring system changes on the second hole, the participants need to shift their focus from their own swing, to playing the game with different rules, to coaching their partner. This would be very difficult for even a professional player. For the beginner or nongolfer, it is very easy to lose focus. Ariel, for example, quickly chose to be the raker. In that role, she doesn't need to focus on golf. As we hear in business every day, its not her job. For Ron, his existing swing and the normal rules of golf are instinctive, so he can focus on playing the game. He can easily ignore Ariel and focus, as he did on the first hole, on making par.

Borrowing a shot from me is a joy for most of the participants because they can, for that swing, let go of the focus on their own swing. It is very relaxing, if for only one moment.

With that perspective in mind, let's find out what's happening on the course. I caught up with Ron and Ariel on the fourth tee. They were looking at the scoring format sheet. "Who made up this stupid scoring system?" Ron asked me.

Why is it that people always judge the people who make up the rules as stupid? Must not know much about being a leader? I thought to myself.

"Stupid? Why do you think it's stupid?" I asked.

"We used the scramble on two and I made a birdie and it turns into a bogey because of the two stroke-penalty on the scoring formula. We just used the all play thing and made a 6.2. That's stupid," he asserted. "Do we round up or down."

He's right. The scores in the all play format could end in a decimal, but generally it doesn't matter. I ignored his comment about the scoring system by asking, "What do you mean, *you* made a birdie? Didn't any of the others play?" I asked.

"Yeah, but only my shots were used," he said. "Okay, *we* made a birdie. Who made up this scoring system?" he asked.

"I did," I said. Ron was silent so I offered, "If you really think about what you are doing, you'll find out that it's brilliant. Your group can make a hole in one on the par 3s." I tried to give him a clue about the strategy of the total group scoring possibilities, but he was focused on blaming the scoring system. Now that he knew I created it, he realized that he was accusing me of being stupid.

"Well, I can see how that approach is good, but we shouldn't be penalized for the scramble format," he said.

"That depends on the strategy in you group," I said. Once again the total group clue went over his head.

Words have different meanings. What I meant by group was not the same as they were thinking. Wally has it figured out. I wonder why he didn't tell them. It would be so simple. Oh well that's why they're out here. They'll figure it out tomorrow, then he'll feel stupid, I thought to myself.

I like to give the participants hints. They can't process them because they are not focused on the strategy of the total group. They are focused on their own foursome. That's the way it is at work—the bunker mentality.

"Say that again?" asked Ariel. "I don't understand how we can make a hole in one?"

"Look at the alternate shot scoring format. If you hit the ball on the green on a par 3, make the putt for a birdie, subtract one, you have a one," I said. "This is a par 3. Why don't you try it here?" I added.

Ron proceeded to tee up his ball. He was going to go first. I interrupted him by saying, "Think carefully about what you are doing. It might be better for someone else to go first," I said.

"I'm the only one who has any chance of hitting the green," he sarcastically replied.

"Really? What about Ariel? If she Swings to Balance, she could do it," I suggested.

"Me, hit the green! No way," Ariel defensively asserted. "I can't hit it that far."

"It's only 125 yards. I saw you hit one that far on the range. Why can't you do it again?" I asked. "Maybe you just don't *trust your swing* yet. Have you been coaching her, Ron?" I asked.

"Coach me? He stopped coaching me on the driving range. He's been too busy trying to impress us with how good he is," she cynically suggested.

That brought an angry reaction from Ron, and before he could say a thing I quickly added, "Well maybe you should be coaching him as well. Help him with the strategy on the hole. That's part of coaching," I suggested. "That's what this is all about."

"We need to get going," said Bryan. "Arguing will not get us to the next hole. What are we going to do?"

"Remember, you can borrow a stroke from me at any time. Think about that possibility?" I suggested.

"Yeah. I can have Bill hit for me. He can hit the green then you can make the putt," Ariel said as she switched her focus from fighting Ron to playing the game.

"Okay, go ahead," Ron said. He was still angry and probably was going to stay that way for a while. To him it was getting stupider by the moment.

I teed up the ball and coached them by saying, "Use your pre-shot routine to imprint Balanced Finish in your mind." I stepped behind the ball, took two Swing to Balance swings the way we showed them on the range, stepped up to the ball and said, "Now coach me. Tell me to Swing to Balance."

"We coach you?" Ariel asked. "You're a pro? Why do you need coaching?"

I stepped back and said, "You'll hear the caddies on TV tell the players to make a smooth swing. That's to help them focus on the swing rather than the distance of the shot. Once the distance is determined and the proper club is selected, the only thing that matters is a smooth swing. Everyone needs coaching," I said. "Let's try it again. This time coach me when I'm ready."

Ariel interrupted and asked, "Do you have the right club?"

I laughed and said, "I have a pitching wedge. It is my 125 yard club. Good question Ariel." I repeated the pre-shot routine from behind the ball, stepped up to the ball, and Ariel said "Swing to Balance, Bill."—*Crack*—the ball headed right at the green and landed two feet from the flag.

"Great shot!" screamed Ariel. "We can make a hole in one!"

Since Bob's group wasn't finished with the third hole, I drove over to the green to watch Ron's group attempt the putt for the one. Ron was about to try the putt when Ariel suggested, "Why don't we let Bryan putt it. The worst thing that can happen is we'd make a two."

Ron relented and Bryan missed the putt. Ron didn't say a thing but I could see the smoke coming from his ears. *Wait until the ninth hole,* I thought.

"I'm sorry," Bryan said.

"Hey, we made a birdie," Ariel said. "That was my tee shot. I'm going to tell everyone I made a birdie."

"What's this I thing all of a sudden?" Ron cynically asserted. "Bill corrected me so let me coach you. This is a we thing, remember."

"I'm glad you finally understand that," Brad asserted. He hadn't said much so far. "It's time we start to think differently about what we're doing. Bill just gave us all the clues we need. If I were investigating a crime, I heard that we are a group, not a foursome. That makes us a part of the total group—all of us together," he said. There was a slight silence and Brad continued, "Bill said we should think about our strategy rather than argue and blame. We better figure out what this is all about before it is too late."

"Typical attorney thinking," Ron said in a sarcastic way. "If we listened to all your legal advice, we would never sell anything. We made a birdie using the alternate shot format, but we can only use it two more times. We have to use the all play deal and we'll get killed on those holes."

"Wait a minute, Ron," Bryan said. "We're in this thing too. If we Swing to Balance, we may do pretty well. Don't think negative. There must be something here we don't see yet," he added.

I laughed to myself and thought, *Are you ever right. Wait till nine.* I got in my cart and said, "If you need another shot, I'll be back again soon. I need to go back to the tee and show the other groups how to make a hole in one."

I arrived back at the tee to greet Bob and the Chairman. "How you doing?" I asked.

"Pretty good. This is harder than we thought. Who made up this scoring system?" the Chairman asked.

"I did. That's the same question Ron asked me. Like it?" I asked.

"Not bad. We made a birdie on that par 5 using that alternate shot format. Wish we could cheat like this in real life," he added.

"Why do you see it as cheating? Sometimes the scoring system in the new business environment is to the distinct advantage of those who know how to Swing to Balance," I said.

"What format are you going to use here?" I asked. "Ron's group just made a birdie on this hole," I added.

That clue went totally over their head. They still think they are competing with the other groups. Wait till they find out, I thought to myself.

"You mean they are beating us?" Bob asked.

"No. All I'm suggesting is maybe you should think carefully about your strategy," I suggested.

"I don't get it," Bob said. "Let's try the all play here. It's a short par 3, no water. We ought to be able to do okay with that format."

"Remember, you can borrow a shot from me at any time. Need any help Wally?" I asked.

"No. I'm going to save you for later. Not sure where, but I'll bet there will be a more strategic time."

Wally has the orange ball thing figured out. At least he knows there is something strategic about it, I thought to myself. *I wonder if he still has the orange ball?*

The coaching wasn't going well in this group. Cheryl was Wally's coach. Wally decided to go first and no one said a word to him, so I asked, "Is anyone going to coach him?"

Cheryl looked at me and said, "He's uncoachable. All he does is write in that manual."

"Let's try it." I took charge and helped Wally by saying, "Take two practice swings." I adjusted Wally to Balance Finish both times. "He's going to need your help," I suggested. No one seemed interested in helping Wally so I said "Ready Wally?" he nodded. "Set-up—Swing to Balance—Swing to Balance—now trust your swing—*Crack*—look at that—on the green. Great shot, Wally!"

Wally was thrilled and gave me a high five. Cheryl ignored him. *There must be some old baggage between Wally and Cheryl,* I thought.

"Better write that one down in your manual, Wally," Bob laughed. "You won't hit another one that good again in your life."

People really hold grudges. I wonder what Wally has done to deserve this treatment? I thought.

Wally thought about what Bob had said while Frank, Bob, and Cheryl hit their tee shots. Then he said to me, "He'll regret that." And he walked away toward the green. He wouldn't get in the cart with Cheryl.

"Wally, come back here," Bob yelled.

I watched from the tee as Wally intentionally four-putted. *I wonder how a guy like Wally tolerates it. It must be miserable knowing the answer and being unable to communicate it to the CEO. Oh well, they'll find out in the end. Maybe it will all change for Wally because of Swing to Balance,* I thought.

I was in a trance thinking about what was happening to Wally when Al's group arrived. "How you doing?" I asked.

"Who invented this game?" Ralph protested.

"What's wrong?" I asked.

"Took us forever to play that par 5. The all play format is a killer," Al added. "Ralph had a fourteen. We're out of it now."

"I wouldn't be so sure. Ron's group made a bogey on that hole and a two here," I said.

"Told you he'd win," Ralph said in a disgusted voice. "This deal just isn't fair for the nongolfers. We can't compete!" he said in a defeated way.

"What makes you think you are competing?" I asked.

There was a quizzical look on Al's face. Ralph quickly argued, "When there's money involved, there's competition."

"Money certainly makes the pro tournaments competitive," I agreed. "Is it always that way in business?" I asked.

There was no answer. "Well, think about your strategy on this hole," I suggested. "Ron's group made a two. You could make a one with the alternate shot format. Have you tried it yet?" I asked.

"A one? How can we make one?" Ralph protested.

"If the first person hits it on the green and the second person makes the putt -- minus one equals a hole in one. You could get your name in the paper," I explained.

They looked at the scoring formula again. "Oh, I see," said Al. "Let's go for it."

"Remember, you can borrow a shot from me at any time. I knocked it in two feet for Ron's group. Bryan missed the putt or they would have had a one." They still didn't understand. So I said jokingly, "If I knock it in the hole, you could have a zero."

Ralph flipped his ball at me and said, "Here, let's see it."

Luckily I caught the ball. It was all beat up from the thrashing on the par 5.

"Been working this one over pretty hard," I laughed.

"Just like he treats his people," Al added.

I quickly said, "If you learn to Swing to Balance, this won't happen. Have you been coaching him Al?" I asked.

"No. He's uncoachable," Al smugly suggested.

"Well let's try it here. The likelihood of a zero is pretty slim, and Ron's group already has the birdie. Let's do this." I gave Ralph a new ball from my pocket. "Come here Ralph. Take a practice swing and hold the finish." Ralph swung and was short of Balanced Finish. I adjusted him to the Balanced Finish position and said, "Feel your body. Do it again." This time he was close to Balance. "Do it one more time." This time he was in Balance. "Now step-up to the ball and Swing to Balance and let the club do all the work." *Crack*—"Great shot!—about ten feet from the flag," I said. "See what a little coaching can do?"

There was silence. Then Al said, "I'm sorry Ralph." There was a long pause, then Al said, "We need to learn to let go while we're out here today. I should have been coaching you."

"Hey guys, don't be sorry today. You came here to learn new leadership skills. The muscle memory of your old game is strong. Go make that putt and have some fun," I coached them to move on.

"Why don't you come and make the putt for us?" Al said.

"The thrill of the hole in one should be yours, not mine," I suggested. "Coach each other. If you make the putt, you'll never forget the experience." I got in my cart and drove off to find Tina's group

Tina's group had just started the second hole. As I approached Tina said, "We're having fun. We don't need your help, right now. Come back in a couple more holes."

"Great," I said and I decided to the find Ron's group again. By now they must be on the sixth hole. As I cruised past Al and Ralph, Al yelled, "We made the putt! A hole in one!"

"Keep coaching. Swing to Balance," I yelled.

As I approached the sixth hole, I could see dad frantically waving to me. He was laughing so hard he couldn't talk. "You gotta see this," he said.

The Chairman was covered with mud. "What happened? I asked.

This is Al. You'll need to wait on the story about the mud. It is funny. I learned a very important leadership lesson on that hole. Ralph and I were in a contest of wills as to who would prove they were right for being a jerk. We were both carrying a grudge and self justified in our bunkers. I wouldn't coach him and he wouldn't coach me. Why? Neither of us has a good answer other than because. We are both visionless slobs playing a game neither of us knows why and we will both lose in the end. Does that make sense? The answer is not only no but hell NO!

When did we learn to be this way? We both know that this isn't mature behavior. We both know that this doesn't lead to productive working relationships within the company, but we keep the war going thinking somehow we will win at the other's expense. It was time to say I'm sorry and quit the game. Right there, after watching Bill help Ralph experience the thrill of a great Swing to Balance shot, I realized how Tom had helped me that day on the range and how I felt. What if we focused on helping each other experience the thrill of winning rather than constantly defending the old game? What is this old game anyhow? How can it be so difficult to defeat?

I made the putt for the one. What a thrill! I'm glad Bill didn't putt it for us. The hole in one created a new relationship between Ralph and me. I can't ever remember being happy for Ralph and he can't ever remember being happy for me. But at that moment we were happy for each other.

Why couldn't we hear the clues? Bill was trying to tell us something and we couldn't hear it. What is the filter? I'll bet our customers are giving us clues and we aren't listening to them either. We may have already lost and not know it. What was Bill trying to tell us when he says Ron's group already made the birdie. That just makes us mad and defeats us more. That can't be the reason he's telling us that.

I wondered how Ron and Ariel were doing. I wanted to stop playing and go tell them to get over it! The old game is an addiction. It is time to declare that we must learn to Swing to Balance together. It's starting to make sense. I hope we all get covered with mud. Maybe we will never forget this day. I hope we get the point of Trust your Swing, daddy. My wife and son have been telling me that for four months now.

I'm not completely sure what I need to do yet, but I know I need to change my game. Stay tuned, it gets very interesting. Awareness precedes change. I am now aware! The Chairman is about to become aware!

Chapter 17
Integrity Matters

Hi, this is Bill. I hope you are having as much fun reading about the Simulation as I am watching the participants make the business connections on the golf course. Al will never forget what he learned on the last hole and the Chairman will never forget the lesson he is about to learn.

I arrived at the sixth hole where the mud bath for the Chairman had occurred. He was a mess, but he was laughing. "What happened?" I asked.

Bob was laughing so hard he couldn't talk. His shoes were off and his pants legs were rolled up. Wally was a little wet and Cheryl was the only one that was dry. There was a pond in front of the sixth green.

"We were playing the alternate shot thing," the Chairman said. "Cheryl hit our second shot. It skipped across the water and hit the bank on the other side. We could see it but thought it might be unplayable so Wally hit a provisional ball. He duffed it three feet," Bob laughed uncontrollably. The Chairman continued, "Bob hit the provisional ball again and hit it up there on the green. See it?" He pointed to a ball on the green about twenty feet from the flag.

Bob picked up the story and said, "When we came around to the green, we found Cheryl's first shot right there in the water. Half the ball was showing so we decided to play it. That's when all hell broke loose." Everyone was laughing so hard they couldn't speak.

Dad continued to tell me the story. "You should've seen it. Cheryl hit the ball in the water, so Wally was next. He carefully tried to chip it out and the ball hit the bank and bounced back in the water. It was now an inch underwater."

I laughed, "Water is impossible to chip from. You have to blast it," I said.

"As we found out," Wally said pointing to his wet pants.

Dad went on, laughing as he tried to tell what happened next. "Bob told Wally to hit it again, and I said wait! It's alternate shot. It's your turn Bob. You should have seen the look on Bob's face when he realized he had just committed himself to the water. Bob said, my turn? I'm not going in the water. What are our options?"

Dad explained what happened next. He told them the ball in the water was in play and they needed to play it or declare it unplayable and go back to the fairway and hit it from there. "They figured they would be hitting five from the fairway and Bob was ready to pick up and go back," dad said.

"Yeah, that's when Frank 'coached me' to hit it out of the water," Bob protested. "He said I didn't have any guts if I didn't try it." Bob laughed so hard he couldn't talk.

"So what happened?" I asked.

"Bob took off his shoes, waded in, and took a big swing. The ball hit the bank again and this time rolled down on that little patch of weeds right there." Dad pointed to the weedy spot.

"Frank said that's enough and was going to pick up the ball and go back to the fairway, but Bob said oh no you're not! It's your turn wise guy. It's my turn to coach you. You should have seen the look on Frank's face." Dad laughed, "It was his turn and no way to avoid the water."

"The first two shots were just water, but the one from the weeds was mud," Bob added.

"Did you get it out?" I asked Frank. "Yes. It's up there on the green. The one with all the mud on it." Everyone laughed.

"Great shot!" I said. It was funny. Everyone except Cheryl was wet and the Chairman was covered with mud. "I'm glad you're having fun."

As they walked toward the green, the Chairman announced they were going to play Bob's provisional ball because it was closer to the flag. He picked up the muddy ball without marking it and began to walk toward Bob's ball.

"You can't play that ball," I said.

The Chairman looked at me and asked, "Why not?" in a rather intimidating tone.

"You can't play a provisional ball on a water hazard. The muddy ball is in play and you have a two stroke penalty for picking it up without marking it," I said.

"Really?" Wally said in a surprising tone.

All of a sudden the mood changed dramatically from laughter and fun to serious business. "I'll explain it later, but you better play on. The next group is waiting in the fairway," I added.

Bob still had his shoes off. His pants were soaked. I could tell that Frank was mad about the penalty for not marking the ball. He flipped the muddy ball at Bob and went over to the cart to get another towel. He was a mess. Bob cleaned the ball and as he replaced it he said, "Let's see, it's your turn again Cheryl."

Cheryl's putt was way short. Wally went next and tapped the ball only two inches. Bob was furious. "Wally! Why did you do that?"

Wally said calmly, "It doesn't matter."

Bob was so mad he missed the remaining five footer. The ball stopped two inches short of the cup. The Chairman was next. He borrowed Bob's putter and hit the ball off the green toward the carts and said, "That's a gimme. What a disaster."

I walked to where the ball was lying on the edge of the green and said, "Why did you do that?" I asked.

"Do what?" Frank asked.

"Hit it off the green. Why didn't you tap it in?"

"That was a gimme," Frank quickly protested.

"A what?" I asked.

"A gimme. It was only two inches," he said in a very irritated manner.

I looked at Dad and he nodded to go on. "I know what a gimme is in a friendly round of golf, but we're playing by USGA Rules today. There is no such thing as a gimme in the rulebook. Your group is lying thirteen right here. That includes a two-stroke penalty for playing with a borrowed club," I said.

All of a sudden, the seriousness of the situation hit Bob. "He's right Frank."

"Oh, come on!" Frank protested.

"If this is about business, we can't cheat and expect to get away with it," Bob suggested.

"There is a lot of money at stake. I wouldn't want you to sign an incorrect score card and be disqualified," I added.

Frank was not a happy camper. Cheryl realized that they had to finish the hole. She chipped it on. Once again Wally tapped it two inches. Bob almost made the next putt, leaving another two-inch tap in for Frank. He glared at me and said, "Okay, I get it. There is no gimme!" and he tapped it in.

Bob tried to smooth it over by saying, "The pros play it all the way out. I guess we should play like the pros."

"But that's a seventeen!" Frank protested. "That kills our chances!"

"Don't forget to subtract the one for the alternate shot format. The official score is a sixteen," I said.

"Oh big deal," the Chairman said. "Like it really matters now!"

"It does matter," Wally said. "If it's a total group game, our official score has to be right or we'll get disqualified. Some other group will do better than sixteen on this hole, but we may have the best score on another hole."

Bob looked at Wally and said, "What are you saying?"

"I've been trying to tell you all day. It's a total group deal, all sixteen of us. It isn't just our score that matters," Wally explained.

Bob looked at me and asked, "Is Wally right?"

"Just suppose he is. What will you do differently on the next hole?" I asked. They were holding up the course and I urged them to move on.

I could see Bob thinking. "Do this," I suggested. "Select a strategy based on both possibilities. Assume it is your group against the others, and then assume it is a total group thing as Wally suggests. How would your strategy change?"

"I'm not sure," Bob said.

All of a sudden Frank came to his senses and said, "If it a total group deal, we'd better make sure one of the last two group makes a par on this hole."

"How would you let them know that, and how would you convince them to trust your thinking?" I asked.

"Why don't you go tell them?" Frank suggested to me.

"I'm just the golf pro. That's not my role," I said.

"Why don't we write them a note and put it on the next tee," Wally suggested.

"Too late for that," Bob protested. "We're probably already dead,"

Bob was right. If it was a total group game, the die was already cast and the only way they could win was by accident. The same is true in business. Every customer service process requires a total group effort even though many companies think it is Sales against Manufacturing against Engineering. They play the old game of hit the numbers and it is an accident if they win together, I thought. *Oh well that's why they're here. They'll never forget that Swing to Balance is a total group game.*

As Frank's group teed off and drove away, I looked at Dad and said, "I hope I didn't make him mad."

"That was terrific," Dad said. "He may be mad, but he'll never forget that lesson."

Dad needed to go to the ninth hole before Ron's group got there, so he drove off toward the ninth tee. Al's group was now walking onto the green. "What was the delay?" Al asked. "Looked like the Chairman was upset about something?"

"He got in the mud. They made a sixteen. I'm sure you'll hear about it later. It was both funny and sad to watch," I added. "How are you guys doing?" I asked.

"We got this game figured out," Ralph said proudly.

"After you showed Ralph how to Swing to Balance, he's been playing lights out," Al added. "Having that one on the score card put us back in the game."

"It is contagious. Once one player elevates their game, the others gain confidence just by watching it work for someone else," I suggested. "It's like the pro tour. When Tiger plays well, it elevates everyone's game."

"I'll bet there is a business principle in there somewhere?" Al joked.

"Think that one through carefully. If your biggest competitor elevates their game to Mass Customization, you'll have no choice but to figure out how to keep pace," I said

"I thought you were only a golf pro?" Al joked.

"I'm here for the golf, but remember, the Simulation is about your business," I added. "Anyone need to borrow a shot? I probably won't see you again until the ninth hole."

"In that case, hit this putt for me," Al said.

"Pros don't hit putts. They stroke the ball with the putter. If you Swing the Putter in Balance, the ball will go in the hole," I added.

"Swing to Balance applies to putting too?" Al asked. "You didn't teach us that."

"Sure. Balance is important to everything in golf." I lined up Al's putt. It was about fifteen feet, right to left break. I swung the putter and the ball went in.

"Amazing! You make it look so easy," Ralph said.

"It is easy once you understand the physics of it. It's like leadership," I added. "What did that give you on the hole?"

"That's a five, minus the one, gives us a four. Way to go Bill!" Ralph said.

"That's great, the group will need that score on this hole."

Al looked at me and said, "Now I'm convinced this is a total group deal. That's the third time you implied that. Am I right?"

"Could be?" I said and I told them the same thing I told Bob and Frank. "Think about your strategy both ways on the next tee. How would you play the game differently if it was a total group deal and how would you communicate to the other groups what you have discovered?" I asked.

"Well, it probably doesn't matter for the groups in front of us. They've already played the game the wrong way. We can tell Tina's group. They're behind us. Are we right? Is it a total group deal?" Al asked anxiously.

"How is it in business?" I asked. "Swing to Balance," I encouraged and I drove off to see how Tina's group was doing.

This is Al. Do you know how it feels to think you have it figured out but you aren't sure you're right. All the clues pointed to a total group deal, but we finally figured it out in the middle of the round and it's too late. That's what we do at work every day. We charge ahead without thinking and find out when it's too late that the game we're playing is wrong. Start with the end in mind is starting to make sense. That's so simple. We know it, but we don't do it. Why?

All of a sudden Ralph and I have a very different reason to cooperate. We both know the secret of the Simulation and don't know how to tell anyone. Little did we know that Wally had it figured out before we started and didn't tell anyone.

Now I'm really frustrated. I'm thinking about how to play my game, coaching Ralph, and worrying about how the total group is doing. I can't focus. This is just like it is at work every day. I try to focus on my job, then Ron calls with a sales problem. I have to coach my people and it wears me out every day.

Why didn't we all think about this on the driving range? I wonder what else we missed on the driving range? I wonder if Bill gave us any clues that went over our heads then? Good thing this is a Simulation. We won't die. Maybe we'll learn something from this that will help us in real life. I'll bet it has something to do with Trust your Swing, daddy. That was the clue I missed.

I'm so glad the Chairman got muddy. Serves him right. I had not heard about the gimme altercation he had with Bill, but that serves him right too. We all cut corners at work. We cheat the customer a little bit every time we cut costs and we think we're getting away with it. Sooner or later someone needs to hand us the rulebook and make us play by the customers' rules. There are no gimmes in their rule book. Quality must be there even in the little details.

I'll bet you can see the business principles while you are reading. We could not see them while we were in the Simulation, but we sure got them after we were done.

Stay with us. It gets worse for us, hopefully better for you.

Chapter 18
Total Commitment

This is Bill. I'll continue to narrate for you until the ninth hole. The altercation with Frank, the Chairman, was very difficult for me. I don't like conflict, but as a golf professional, I had to learn to play by the rules regardless of the consequences. The integrity of the game is more important than any one player. Likewise, in business, the integrity of the company is more important than the quarterly executive bonus or stock price. That lesson for Frank may be the most important thing that happens for these people today. We'll find out later.

After the mud bath, I turned my attention to Tina's group. They were nowhere in sight, so I hurried back to find them. They were so far behind I thought they had quit. I found them still on the second hole and they appeared to be struggling. As I approached, I could see Sharon in a sand trap. I watched from a distance so they wouldn't be embarrassed. Three swings later she picked up the ball and tossed it on the green. I laughed to myself, thinking about all the people who I had taught how to get out of the sand. It is one of the most difficult things for beginners to learn.

"Need some help?" I asked, as I drove up to the green.

"Where've you been? We can't get out of that sand," Sharon said.

"Be nice," I cautioned. "The golf gods will hear you and you'll be condemned to sand purgatory forever," I laughed. "Sand is tough stuff, but it's better than water," I added.

"You can say that again! Do you have any more balls? I fed the water monster big time on this hole," Sharon said.

There is a lateral water hazard in the middle of the dogleg of this hole, but it is a long way out of play for good players. I looked and Tina didn't have the orange ball in her hand so I asked her, "Did the orange ball bring you good luck?"

"No," she said. "I retired it when we came around that water."

I wasn't sure what she meant but assumed that *retired it* meant she lost it. Oh well. "How are you doing with the new scoring format?" I asked.

"We decided to use the all play thing here. We're over the twelve shot limit, but we're having fun. We figured we couldn't beat Ron, and we all wanted to play all the way out to see how bad we really are."

"We're having a lot of fun coaching each other," Sharon said. "It's the blind leading the blind. You know, *Trust your Swing, Tina,*" she laughed at Tina.

"That's good," I suggested. "You'll need that later. I saw you use the hand wedge out of the sand." I laughed and pointed to the trap beside the green.

"Hand wedge? Oh, throwing it, you mean? We've done lots of that. It's the only way to get out of those things," Sharon laughed.

"We're having fun rather than trying to win the money," Mark added. "We decided to not worry about the business thing—you know—the money," he added. "That's way out of reach."

"What if the people who work for you told you that? How would that make you feel?" I asked. They were silent for a moment, not understanding what I had just asked. So I added, "You know—the money thing. What if everyone was having fun but the money thing was being ignored?" I asked.

There is always some justification for the lack of focus in business. They thought for a moment and Mike said, "We watched Ron drive the green on one. If we all hit our best shots and put them together, we couldn't hit it that far. There's no way we can compete with him."

"Where docs it say you are competing with him?" I asked.

That question prompted them to pause and think for a moment. Then Sharon said, "If there is money on the line, Ron will compete!" she asserted.

"I know. I've watched him, but he is dependent on his group for winning, and it will eventually come down to Ariel's ability," I said.

They thought for a moment and Sharon confidently assured everyone, "He'll find a way around her."

"Then you've decided to quit and stay is that right?" I asked.

"Quit and stay? What do you mean by that?" Sharon protested.

"A lot of people figure out that they don't make a big contribution to the success of a company. When they are convinced that what they do doesn't matter, they do what is called quit and stay. They draw a paycheck, do what they're told, but don't see that they are involved in the strategic agenda of the organization. They survive by being quiet and not confronting people like Ron for the way he plays the game. They tolerate the abuse," I said. "I guess dad hasn't covered what it means to quit and stay, with you yet. Has he?" I asked.

"No, but we're still here. We haven't quit," Mike protested.

"You quit playing the game of the Simulation and stayed here playing golf," I suggested.

"Oh, I see what you mean. But we can't beat Ron," he protested again.

"Maybe you don't have to beat Ron. Have you really thought carefully about your strategy?" I asked.

"Well, I guess we haven't. We decided after watching Ron on the first tee that it didn't matter," Tina suggested. "We haven't even figured out what a scramble means."

"Putt out and we'll get you back in the business game on the next hole. I'll help you."

Dad has told me about the legions of quit and stay people who work in organizations. He suggested that I use that terminology if I ever encounter people who feel defeated before they start. It seems to have worked with Tina's Group, I thought. At least it got their attention.

The group assembled on the third tee and Sharon said, "Okay, we're committed. What should we do?"

"Well, the first step is to realize that your participation in the Simulation is important. You must participate to be successful." I could not tell them it was a total group game, but I could help them think about the strategy. "Remember, you can all borrow a shot from me, and I can hit it as far as Ron. So, he doesn't have an advantage over you." They listened intently.

"Now, look at the three formats. Using the alternate shot format, you can score a one on some holes. If you Swing to Balance, we can hit the green on a par 3, make the putt, subtract one and you have a hole in one. If you use the alternate shot format on a par 5, reach the green in two and make an eagle, that's a two."

"What's an eagle?" Sharon asked

I laughed and said, "I'm sorry. An eagle is two under par on any hole. It would be a two on a par 4 or a three on a par 5," I added.

"Have you ever made one?" she asked.

"Lots of them," I suggested. "And from the tees we are playing today, I can easily reach all the par 5s in two, and I can drive the green on this hole. By strategically using your support resource, you can put some low scores on the card. Want to try it?" I asked.

"Sure!" they all eagerly yelled.

"Okay, raise you right hand and repeat after me." They raised their hands and I said, "We are committed to playing the game to the finish."

"We are committed to playing the game to the finish," they all repeated with enthusiasm.

And I said, "Our participation really matters."

"And our participation really matters," they echoed.

"We will Swing to Balance!" I added.

"We will Swing to Balance!" They all laughed.

"I'm not going to help you unless you are committed," I suggested. "And I don't want you to think Swing to Balance is a laughing matter. It will be a very serious command before it is all over," I cautioned. "We need to use it on every shot from here out."

Tina had no idea at this time how important that pledge would be, but I knew what was in store for her on the ninth hole. If they weren't committed to Swing to Balance, it would be a disaster.

The mood turned from fun to serious. They were now focused on playing the game. "I didn't mean to deflate the fun mood," I suggested. "But a Professional

Golfer must focus during a tournament. Okay, who's shot should I use first?" I asked. It really didn't matter but I wanted it to be their choice.

"Use mine," Tina said.

From the tees we were playing, the next par 4 was only 240 yards. That's a comfortable three wood for me. *No trouble in front of the hole—just a bunker to the left of the green,* I thought. They watched as I teed up the ball. I stepped back and went through the Swing to Balance pre-shot routine. I looked at them and said, "Coach me."

"Trust your Swing, Billy. Swing to Balance," came the response. *Crack—* "Get on!" I yelled as the ball headed toward the green. It landed on the green and stopped ten feet from the hole.

"That's amazing!" Tina said. "My dad used to hit them that way."

Was your dad a pro?" I asked.

"No, but he was a good player," she added.

"Let's go. We're way behind." I jumped in my cart and took off toward the green. I chuckled to myself. *That was not only amazing, it was one of the best three woods I'd hit in a long time. Nice to have it happen at this time. Too bad dad didn't see it. I thought. He'll love this story. I wondered how the rest of the groups were doing and whether Ron and Ariel had reached the ninth hole yet. That will be a disaster.*

They ran up on the green. The serious mood had turned to excitement. "If we make this putt we'll have a one, right?" Mark asked.

"That's right," I said.

"Use my shot. You make the putt," he suggested.

"Let's think about it," I suggested. "Maybe you should save my shots for the long ones. It would be nice to make this putt, but it would be okay to two-putt. That would give you a two. I can easily miss this putt. It has a big break so it can be missed. We definitely don't want to three-putt. So what do you think? Who's the best putter?" I asked.

"Mark's can putt real good," Tina said.

"Okay. Mark you putt it and we'll save Bill's shots for the long ones. Sound good team?" Tina asked.

I helped Mark line up the putt and he just missed. Mike tapped the next putt in and they were excited. "That's amazing. A two on a par 4," Tina said.

The excitement level continued to grow. "We're back in it!" Mike said. The accountant in him had just figured it out.

"No more quit and stay for us. Look out Ron, here we come!" Sharon added.

The next hole was a par 3. "What do you think?" I asked. It was important that they think through the strategy. It is easy for me, but they must decide.

"Let's do the same thing," Sharon suggested. "You hit my shot and we can make the putts."

"That assumes that I'll hit the green," I added "How about the scramble format. If three people hit and someone doesn't hit the green, then you can borrow a shot from me. Just make sure the last person isn't Tina. I've already hit for her."

They decided to use the scramble format. Mark went first and hit his shot right at the pin. It looked like it could have gone in the hole. "That's amazing! Great shot!" I exclaimed.

"Let's go play that one. We won't get one closer than that," Tina said, starting to leave the tee box.

"Wait." I stopped her and suggested, "This is a good time for you to practice your swing. I haven't seen you swing since the driving range. Let's try the Swing to Balance swing. You might need it later." She agreed and I helped her like I had helped Ralph and Wally. Tina was athletic and could Swing to Balance fairly well.

"Okay, try it for real," I suggested. They all played to the green even though Mark's ball was close to the pin. Tina swung the club and hit a great shot that landed just short of the green but it was straight. "Great swing," I said. Sharon had trouble balancing and missed the ball completely. Mike was a decent player. He used too much club and hit it over the green on the fly. "Great swing! You really got into that one," I laughed.

"Yeah this Swing to Balance thing has given me more distance," he said. "It's hard to judge the distances of my clubs now," he added.

Mark's ball was three feet from the hole. A great shot. The putt was straight in. "Since you are using the scramble format, you have four chances at it. Tina who should go first?" I asked.

"I'll try it. We'll save Mark for last."

Tina made the putt. You would have thought she had won the lottery. She pumped her fist like Tiger Woods and yelled, "Just like on TV. We're in it now. A hole in one!"

I said, "Not so fast. Look at the scoring formula for the scramble. The scramble scoring format doesn't subtract one. It adds two. That's a four, not a one," I suggested.

The mood quickly turned cold. "Why did you let us use the scramble. You should have told us," They argued.

"I suggested the scramble because Al's group made a one here. It was a good chance for you to use up one of the scramble formats and save the alternate shot format for the tough holes ahead."

"This doesn't make any sense," Sharon added. "We make four, they make one, and we should be happy? I don't get it." She was angry.

Tina looked at her and said, "I get it. It's a total group score. They have the one so we didn't need to worry about our score here. We needed to save the alternate shot deal for holes where the total group doesn't do well. Is that right?" she asked, looking at me.

"That's one way to think about it," I said. "Is business a total group thing or independent groups acting alone?" I asked. "Maybe that's the way to resolve it?" I said in a very confirming way.

"I thought you were a golf pro. What do you care about business?" Mark asked.

"The PGA Tour is a business," I suggested. "Every pro needs to understand how his or her behavior impacts the business of Professional Golf," I added.

"We need to know right now how the other groups did on the remaining holes so we can use the alternate shot and Bill's help when the total group needs it. I see it! We're playing a business game. This is not about golf." Tina insisted.

We arrived at the next tee. "Do you know what the other groups made on this hole?" Tina asked.

"I'm not sure. I see the head pro waving at me. I'll catch up with you on the sixth tee," I said as I started toward my cart.

"Wait," Sharon yelled. "You can't abandon us like that."

"You'll be fine. *Trust your swing,*" I said as I drove off.

Eddie, the head pro wanted to know if it was okay to let other groups out on the course yet. I told him the saga of the mud bath and that I was trying to hurry the last group along. He agreed to keep the course closed for another fifteen minutes, but he would have to let the members out by then.

As I returned, I saw Tina's group doing a high five on the fifth green. "What did you make?" I yelled.

They came over to their carts and said, "We used the scramble deal and made a par."

"That's a six on the score card," I said.

"We know, but you should have seen the putt Sharon made. It was at least thirty feet."

Sharon was excited. "What's next?" she yelled.

The next hole was the mud bath hole, a par 4 over the water. I didn't want to tell them about the Chairman until they chose a strategy. "It's a par 4 over water," I said.

"Do you know what the other groups made?" Tina asked.

"Bob's group made sixteen and Al's group made a four. I'm not sure about Ariel's group."

"You mean Ron's group," Sharon suggested. "He probably made a par."

"Then we need a one or two," Mike said. "Let's use the alternate shot format," he asserted.

"How did Bob's group make a sixteen?" Mark asked.

"The Chairman got a mud bath," I said. I told them the story about the shots out of the water. I did not tell them about the gimme. "You'll have to ask them how they made sixteen," I suggested. "It's a funny story."

"Can you hit it over the water," Tina asked.

"From here it's 250 yards to carry the water. It's 270 to the pin. These down tees are nice," I added. "If you coach me to Swing to Balance and the ball goes straight, I can carry the water and possibly get it on the green. It will be close," I assured her. "If I miss it, it could go in the water. No guarantees. It's your choice," I suggested

"Why do we need to coach you? Don't you naturally Swing to Balance?" Tina asked.

"Yes, but it's a matter of focus. Right now I'm still thinking about what the head pro asked me. So you need to be absolutely certain that I am in the present before you let me swing the club," I explained.

"I wish I could stay focused," Sharon said. "My mind always wanders."

"That's why the Swing to Balance command is so important. It gets people to focus on what is really important at that moment. When you learn to Swing to Balance and can trust that everyone is committed, your organization will be confident in serving customers," I suggested.

"Here, hit mine," Sharon said as she offered me her ball.

"No offense, but I'll use a new ball. I want to be sure the ball is perfectly round when I have a critical shot like this. There is very little margin for error," I added.

I took the Swing to Balance practice swings. Stepped up to the ball and said, "Coach me." Swing to Balance was the command. *Crack*—"Go!—Go!—Made it!" I said.

"Is it on the green?" Sharon asked with excitement.

"Not sure. It's close. Let's go find out," I said.

The ball was on the left fringe about twenty feet from the hole. "Great shot!" Even I was excited. That was the second great shot for Tina's group. "What now?" Sharon said. She could hardly contain herself.

"What do you all think? Mark, can you chip as well as you putt?" I asked.

"Sometimes." He paused as he looked at the next shot. "I'd rather putt it from here. Two putts and we have a two, right? And we still have two shots left from you, right?" Mark asked as he figured the potential scoring opportunities.

Unfortunately, they three-putted from the fringe and recorded a three on the scorecard. On the seventh hole, a par 4, I played the drive for Mike. Mark reached the green with an 8 iron and they two-putted for the par 4, net three. Tina was keeping the score card and said with delight, "We're one under par on the last five holes!"

"Keep it going. You've used your borrowed shots very well. You'll need to tell everyone how you did it," I said. "I need to go. I'll see you on the ninth hole."

As I drove past Al's group, they were waving frantically. I stopped but didn't get out of the cart. "What's up?" I shouted.

"Does Tina's group know that it is a total group thing?" Ralph yelled.

"You'll have to ask them," I yelled and drove off. I wanted to get to the ninth hole to see Wally deal with the orange ball. If I hurried, I may be in time for the Ron and Ariel show.

This is Al. Things got better for our group after Ralph and I stopped the old game. We coached each other and actually started having some fun. Bill wasn't around to help us.

After we figured out the total group deal, we drove ahead and told Bob and Frank. They already knew it from Wally. We told them to go up and tell Ron and Ariel and they said they would.

We dropped back and told Tina's group. Sharon still wasn't convinced. She thought there still might be a trick to this thing. She warned us that there still might be a change in the rules on the ninth hole.

How do you convince other people in other divisions that your perspective is right? Sharon obviously doesn't trust us for some reason. I wonder how we can prove it to her out here on the course? Maybe there's no way?

Chapter 19
The Moment of Truth

This is Tom. I'll narrate for the ninth hole. Bill will be busy helping the orange ball players and I wouldn't want you to miss the ninth hole experience. That's what the Simulation is all about.

I saw Bill racing toward the ninth tee so I killed some time with Ron by checking the group's score card to be sure they had played all the different scoring formats.

"What are the rules for this hole?" Ron asked sarcastically. "I sure hope we don't have to play that all play format again," he added.

"What's the matter with it?" I asked. "It prepares you for what's about to happen," I added. He was angry about the eight hole. They had to use the all play format and made a big number. That's all he would tell me.

"How does your group stand?" I asked.

"We're five over, but I'll bet we're in the lead," Ron quickly advised. "If it hadn't been for this stupid scoring system we'd be even."

"What's wrong with the scoring system?" I asked.

"The two stroke penalty on the scramble format is stupid. We made birdies both times we used it and they turn into bogeys. This whole thing is crazy," he said.

"Did you use any shots from Bill?" I asked as Bill arrived at the tee.

"Ariel did. I didn't need to," Ron suggested in an arrogant way. "Bryan and Brad still have one coming. They're going to use Bill here," Ron added.

"Okay. You have another email from the Chairman," I said as I handed them the rules for the ninth hole. "It says that only the score of the orange ball player counts on the ninth hole."

"The orange ball player? What does that mean?" Ron protested.

"One of your players received an orange ball on the first tee. They must play the ninth hole alone and only their score counts," I added calmly knowing that Ariel was now filled with fear.

"Who has the orange ball?" Ron asked in a panic.

"I had it," Ariel said. "But I lost it on the first hole."

"It also says here that failure to bring the original orange ball back to the official scorer is a two-shot penalty," I added.

Ron lost his composure. "What if we ignore the email?" Ron protested. "Forget the Chairman's email! I can easily birdie this hole from here. Now you tell us that only Ariel is going to play this hole. No way!"

"You can quit," I suggested.

This must be what it's like in the boardroom when the Chairman announces that the company has lost money and there must be massive layoffs in order for the Company to survive. There was stunned silence in the group. Ron's protest had turned to internal rage. Ariel was speechless. Brad and Bryan were unable to offer an opinion for fear of infuriating Ron further.

"Have you been coaching Ariel?" I asked. The obvious answer was no. Ron had not paid much attention to Ariel starting on the driving range. She had accepted the role of raker on the first hole. Ron was the hero. He was going to carry the load.

"She's a beginner! How can you expect her to be the only one to play this hole?" Ron continued his protest.

"It's not my decision. It was made by the Chairman," I added. I could see Bill holding back his laughter as he watched the ensuing argument. "You've had all day to prepare her for this moment. What did you expect to happen to the beginners? Sooner or later they must contribute," I suggested. "That time has arrived."

I took charge and said, "Ariel, you are on the tee. You have one minute. Your group is now on the clock for slow play. No more debate," I firmly asserted.

The group assembled with a hopeless look and Brad said, "You can do it Ariel. Just Swing to Balance."

"I haven't been coached all day. Now you want me to Swing to Balance?" Ariel said with an angry look in Ron's direction. "Serves you right. You've been the big shot all day."

I intervened by taking Ariel aside. "You can do it, but you won't succeed if you continue to blame Ron. You are as much responsible for your condition as he is. You must focus on the moment, and we can argue about who is to blame later." I looked her in the eye and said, "Bill will coach you until you get off the tee. Then you must depend on your group. Okay?"

Tears came to Ariel's eyes. I held her shoulders and told her quietly that it was okay to be scared. "You aren't alone. Wally, Ralph, and Tina also have the orange ball. They will face the same challenge." I waited a moment and said, "Come on, I'll ask Bill to help you."

I motioned to Bill and said, "Ariel needs a coach. Will you help her?"

As Bill moved toward Ariel, Ron protested, "I'm her coach." Ariel snapped out of her state of fear and said, "Not now you aren't! We've hired a consultant to take charge."

Everyone could feel the tension. It is a low feeling for any executive to be told that the company is hiring a consultant to do what they have ignored for years.

"I'll help her for the first swing, then you can take it from there," Bill suggested. "She'll need all of you to coach her as she plays the rest of the hole," Bill added.

Everyone watched as Bill coached Ariel. "Take two deep breaths. Get yourself calmed down. I want you to think Swing to Balance three times." Bill looked at Ariel as she took the breaths and concentrated on the Swing to Balance swing thought. "See it in your mind," Bill added.

"Okay. Take a practice swing and hold your finish position," Bill said. Ariel swung what she thought was a Balanced Swing and held her finish. Bill adjusted her up to Balanced Finish position and said, "Do it again and this time try to get to Balance."

"It's hard to do," Ariel said in a determined tone.

"Yes it is," Bill agreed. "Try it one more time. Set-up to the ball and Swing to Balance." Ariel swung to Balance and Bill said, "Okay, you're ready."

The moment of truth had arrived. The entire day had been orchestrated for this moment. Time nearly stood still. I couldn't breath. Ariel took a swing and—whoosh—missed the ball.

"Good swing!" Bill asserted

"She missed the ball!" Ron said from the back of the tee. "Hit the ball!" he yelled.

Bill looked toward Ron and said, "That's why she missed it. She tried to hit it." Bill ignored Ron's protest and focused on Ariel. "Take a practice swing—hold your finish—do it again—feel the wholeness of the swing. Okay, set-up and Swing to Balance," he urged. Once again time stood still as Ariel swung at the ball. *Crack*—The ball went straight off the tee and landed in the fairway.

"I did it!" Ariel screamed and hugged Bill in her excitement.

As Bill looked at me, my eyes began to water. We've both seen this moment many times before, but it's still very emotional. The joy that people experience when they accomplish something for the first time is exciting.

Brad and Bryan were patting Ariel on the back and moving quickly toward their carts. "Let's go!" they shouted.

Ariel was in the cart and Ron was still standing on the tee. "Come on big shot," she yelled. "You're my coach now."

Before he could move, I approached Ron and said, "You need to be concerned about how she feels at this moment. What she does from here on will be a function of how well you keep her focused." Ron glared at me. He was too mad to hear what I had just said. "Did you hear her? She needs a coach."

There was a moment of silence. Ron could see Bob and the Chairman watching. He walked toward the cart, slammed his club in his bag and drove off.

By now both Bob and Al's groups had arrived at the tee. They had seen what had happened but didn't know the orange ball rules. As Ariel's group drove away, Bill came over to me and said, "Another tough lesson. I hope Ron gets it."

I looked at Bill and said, "These are the moments that make our work worthwhile. I think he got it. He just doesn't want to admit it right now. This experience could change his life."

"Let's hope so," Bill said.

I agreed by saying, "You did a great job with Ariel. That wasn't easy."

By now Bob and the Chairman were anxious to know the rules of the ninth hole. The Chairman asked, "What was that all about?"

"You changed the game and it was a very difficult assignment for Ariel," I suggested.

"I did what?" he asked.

I explained the rules for the ninth hole to both groups that had assembled on the tee. Once again the same question was asked, "The orange ball player? What orange ball?" Ralph confessed that he had lost the orange ball on the first hole.

"Why did you play it?" I asked.

"No one told me not to. It was just another ball to me," Ralph suggested.

"How about you Wally?" I asked.

Wally calmly reached in his pocket, produced the orange ball, and said, "I knew there was some significance to this thing. I even wrote it down in my manual." For the first time Wally was in control of his group. Even Cheryl was now paying attention to him.

"There is a point to all this I'm sure?" the Chairman asked in a rhetorical tone.

"Yeah, either tell people in advance about the orange ball or don't change the rules in the middle of the game," Al laughed. "I figured it would all come down to our weakest link sooner or later. Glad it's not me."

The Chairman was not amused by Al's comment. "So all of a sudden it's my fault? Is that it?" he sternly asked.

Once again I intervened before the anger could escalate, "It's not your fault. This email is in response to the changes in the marketplace. When customers change the game, all the old measures of success don't matter. Everyone in the organization needs to be able to Swing to Balance. You can only hope they are prepared when it's their turn."

"I take it Ariel had the orange ball in Ron's group?" Wally asked.

"That's right."

"No wonder Ron was so mad. He probably hadn't prepared her for this moment," Wally said.

"You're right again. How about you? Are you ready?" I asked.

Wally confidently strolled to the tee, placed the orange ball on the tee and was about to hit. "Wait!" screamed Bob "Don't hit that thing! It doesn't say you have to play it. It's a two-stroke penalty for losing it."

Wally looked at Bob, looked at Cheryl, looked at the Chairman, and quietly said, "Now you're paranoid." He proceeded to hit the orange ball with a big slice into the weeds to the right of the fairway.

"Wally, you idiot! Why don't you listen?" Bob screamed.

Wally reached for another ball in silence. I could tell that he was not only mad but was determined to do it again. "Wait," I said. "The weeds are marked as a lateral hazard. If you can't find the orange ball, you drop two club lengths from where it last crossed the hazard. "Frank, you know the lateral hazard rule, right?" The Chairman nodded yes, and they walked toward the carts in silence.

As they drove off, Al yelled, "*Trust your swing, Wally.*"

Bill came over to me and said, "Another lesson learned, I hope?"

I looked at him and said, "The ninth tee is an amazing place."

I looked down the fairway and could see Ariel approaching the water that fronts the ninth green. The ninth hole is a par 5 with a very difficult 100-yard shot over water. I told Bill, "Go help Ariel. She'll need your help."

Bill ran to his cart and drove off toward Ariel and Ron. Wally and his coaches were looking frantically in the weeds for the orange ball. After a few minutes, I saw Wally drop another ball. He took two practice swings under the watchful eye of the Chairman and proceeded to slice the next shot into the weeds again. They moved forward, looked again, and Wally dropped a third ball. I turned to Al and said, "Wait till he gets to the water in front of the green. I hope he gets over his anger before that. He'll have no chance if he's mad."

Al said, "Knowing Wally, he'll quit if Bob yells at him again. As you could see, he gets real mad when people yell at him."

I looked at Al and said, "That's what leadership is all about."

Al was silent. Then he said in a rather humble way, "I don't understand what that means?"

I looked at Al and said, "The success of the total group now depends on Wally making it across the water. Wally must finish the hole regardless of his score."

Al was trying to digest what I had said. I continued, "Al, in business, people quit every day because they are frustrated with the orange ball. The orange ball person is typically in front of a customer when the orange ball experience happens, and they hit the ball in the weeds, as Wally did. When they quit, the senior leaders have convenient excuses, like they're minimum wagers, what do you expect. The process repeats itself over and over again until the company fails. That's a lack of leadership," I said with some conviction.

Al just looked at me. This wasn't the time to explain more about the plight of the orange ball players. It was time for him to experience it, I turned to Ralph and said, "It's your turn."

By now Ralph and Al grasp the seriousness of the situation. Both Ariel and Wally were headed toward disasters. Someone must make a good score with the orange ball. I could see Al bite his lip. I looked at Al and said, "Al, Ralph needs leadership from you right now."

Al looked at me with a very different look. He understood the leadership challenge. He took charge of the situation and said, "Ralph, you're up and you can do it. Remember the fourth hole. You were great and you've been doing it very well since then."

Tina's group arrived in time to see what happened next. Ralph froze. "What's the matter?" Al asked.

Ralph couldn't answer. There was silence. Al patiently said, *"Trust your swing, Ralph.* Just Swing to Balance," Al encouraged.

Ralph teed up the ball. Took two practice swings—stepped up to the ball—set-up. Al firmly said, *Trust your Swing, Ralph. Crack*—Ralph hit a beautiful drive straight down the fairway. "Great swing!" High fives were everywhere.

Extreme tension will often cause people to freeze. I've seen it many times. The brain cannot process a logical command. People often can't remember answers to simple questions. The emotional learning mechanism is very strange.

As they moved toward their carts, Al looked at me in silence. Then he said, "I get it."

I nodded and said, "It's important, isn't it?" Al was unable to talk. "Go help Ralph. He'll need more coaching."

"We're rooting for you Ralph," Tina yelled as they drove away. "Don't forget it's a total group game."

I looked at Tina's group and said, "You're next. Are you ready?"

Tina nodded, but I wasn't sure she knew what was about to happen. At this moment, I could hardly breath. The ninth tee experiences take a heavy toll on my emotional body. All I could do was shake my head. It all started for Al on that day in October and I think he finally understands what *Trust your Swing, daddy* means?

I looked down the fairway and could see Bill helping Ariel. By now, there were three groups on the ninth fairway. Wally was waiting for Ariel to clear the water and Ralph's drive had nearly reached Wally's group. I quickly explained the rules for the ninth hole to Tina's group and told them to wait here. I jumped in my cart to find out what was happening with Ariel.

This is Al. I get it. I now understand the Trust your Swing, daddy command. That's all I could say to Ralph that would make sense. It wasn't logical to say it. It just came out. It was amazing. It worked.

I'm sitting in the cart with Ralph watching the Ron and Ariel show up ahead. Wally and Bob seem to be arguing about something. My temptation is to go tell them to get over it, but at this point nothing will matter. All I can do is make sure Wally finishes the hole if he looks like he's going to quit.

There is probably more to it than this, but it all comes down to the orange ball player. If they aren't prepared for the challenge, it doesn't matter how smart the senior leaders are. It doesn't matter how good of a player Ron is. I can see it all unfolding in front of me on the ninth fairway. Ron is now making gestures toward the water. Wally is just waiting patiently for Ariel's group to get out of the way. Here we are stuck waiting on the Ron and Ariel show. It's so simple, Trust your Swing, Ariel, and it's all about the money. The money will be lost if all the orange ball players don't finish the hole. If you had been in that cart with me at that moment you would understand how to lead you company. It isn't about what you know. It's about the muscle memory of the entire group.

All of a sudden I see Ron take out a club, throw a ball down, and take a practice swing. What is he doing?

Chapter 20
Stay in the Present

I arrived just in time to see Bill consoling Ariel. Ariel had hit four balls in the water. She was distraught and wanted to quit. Bill had given her a clue as to what was happening. He told her it was a total group game and that Ron was the only one who had made a par on the first hole. All of the other groups had double bogeyed that hole. In her emotional state it was difficult for her to understand what Bill was trying to tell her, but it clicked when he said it was important for her to finish the hole regardless of her score.

All of a sudden Ariel screamed to Ron, "Wait! You can't do that. We'll be disqualified if you hit that shot!"

Ron was set-up and ready to hit a shot. Ariel ran toward Ron and yanked the club out of his hand and yelled, "My score doesn't matter at this point. It is your score on one that matters. Get it?" she demanded.

"At this point it doesn't matter," Ron protested. "You've blown it. You're going to make a twenty on this hole if you ever do get it across the water!" he yelled.

"You don't get it," she yelled. "I have to finish the hole or your par on the first hole won't count for the total group."

"It doesn't matter at this point! We're out of it!" Ron yelled back.

Suddenly, Brad, who had been watching the action from his golf cart intervened by saying, "Ron, she's right. You can't hit that ball. Ariel must do it."

Ron backed off as both Brad and Bryan stepped forward. Bill gave them some advice and a minute later I heard, "Swing to Balance Ariel," and her next swing sent the ball over the water and onto the back edge of the green. Ariel was elated. She jumped in the cart with Bill and motioned for him to take her to the green. Bill talked to her for a few moments and drove his cart over to Ron and motioned for Ariel to get out and join Ron. It wasn't a peaceful reunion, but Ariel jumped into the cart with Ron and they drove across the bridge toward the green.

I drove over to Bill and asked, "Another lesson learned?"

"I think so," Bill said. "I told her she is responsible for her own condition and that she must finish the hole regardless of Ron's behavior. I told her a pro must perform regardless of the emotions. I think that helped her see the situation differently."

"That's a tough lesson to teach her under that level of stress," I said.

"That's the best time to learn it, remember?" Bill said.

I nodded as I recalled the number of times that Bill and I had talked about the responsibilities of any professional. There are many times when professionals must perform even though they are not feeling well. The audience doesn't care. They paid money to see the performance and the show must go on.

Bill and I watched from the fairway as Ariel jumped out of the cart, grabbed her putter, and hurried toward her ball. Ron just sat in the cart. Ariel putted the ball toward the hole. Three putts later it was in. She pumped her fist like Tiger Woods and yelled back at us, "I finished!" We both clapped and once again my eyes filled with tears. For her it was an emotional victory. For Ron it was a tragedy. Hopefully, someone will help him understand.

Bill and I turned to watch Wally. He was still angry about his coaching. We motioned for him to hit and he sculled one straight into the water. "Here we go again," Bill said. "If it looks like he's going to quit, I'll handle it the same way I did with Ariel," Bill added.

"Good. I need to go back to the tee and help Tina." I headed back to the ninth tee where Tina's group was waiting. As I drove past Al and Ralph they asked, "How did Ariel do?"

"I have no idea what she scored, but she finished the hole. That's all that matters," I said.

Al looked at me and said, "It's all about the money now, isn't it?"

"The money is very important. Without it there will be no tomorrow," I said.

As I arrived on the tee, Tina asked, "What happened to Ariel?"

"She had a tough time with her coach. He wanted to hit the ball for her," I said in a rather serious tone. "She didn't let that happen and finished the hole. That's all that matters."

Tina had not seen Wally's tee shot. She looked down the fairway and said, "Looks like Wally's having trouble too."

"This is a very difficult hole. There's water in front of the green. Takes about a 100-yard shot to carry it. He'll need better coaching than he's had up until now," I suggested. "Are you ready?"

I went over the rules again. "We've got it figured out," Tina said confidently. "I'm ready. We've been practicing while you were gone. It's just like my dad told me in high school."

"What did he tell you?" I asked.

"He said I need to be prepared for the pressure of the last hole. He made me practice making putts while he was yelling at me. That's why I quit the game. It wasn't any fun, but now I know what he meant," she explained. "You aren't going to yell at me are you?" she laughed.

"The only thing I'll tell you is *Trust your Swing* and Swing to Balance. That's all you need to be thinking," I suggested.

"Let's go gang," Sharon urged.

Tina took two practice swings—approached the ball—then backed off. "What's wrong?" Sharon asked.

"I forgot." Tina said

"Forgot what?" Sharon asked.

"Forgot how to start the swing," Tina said

She looked at me. "It happens to every pro. It's a matter of concentration. You were probably still thinking about your dad," I laughed.

"That's exactly right. How did you know?" Tina asked.

"We can talk about it tomorrow. Stay in the present. Commit to Swing to Balance. Listen to your coaches. Coach her a little more aggressively this time," I suggested to Sharon and Mark. "You must capture her mind."

Tina stepped back and took two practice swings. The coaching came from everyone, "Swing to Balance Tina!" *Crack*—straight and long right down the middle. Sharon was beside herself. She clutched her hands to her mouth gasping for breath. Tina was airborne. Once again, tears came to my eyes. *That's what it's all about,* I thought.

"Amazing!" Sharon screamed.

Tina looked at me and confidently said, "How good was that!"

I couldn't talk. My eyes were filled with tears and I just nodded approval. The emotions of the ninth tee are sometimes overwhelming, even for the spectators. Tina was euphoric and raced to the golf cart, jumped in, and nearly left without Mark. "Let's go make a par!" she shouted as they drove off toward the fairway.

I waited a moment to take it all in. The ninth hole experience is why we conduct the Simulation. I reflected on the four different experiences. What a difference between Ariel, Wally, Ralph, and Tina. *Why does it take so long for some people to let go?* I thought.

I followed Tina's group down the fairway. She selected an iron for her second shot and I watched as she bladed the next one. "At least it went straight," she said.

"Keep it on the short grass," I said and drove on to see how Ralph was doing. By now Ralph was at the water with Bill and Al. Wally had finished the hole with a twenty-two. He wanted to quit, but Ariel had apparently come back to the fairway and told him that he had to finish the hole.

I watched as Ralph made his first attempt to clear the water. It cleared the water but hit the bank in front of the green and rolled back into the water. "What now?" he asked Al and Bill.

"It's a water hazard. You cleared the water but you can't drop over there. So you must hit again from here. You can move up closer to the water if you wish, or you can go back as far as you wish, as long as you keep the point of entry between yourself and the flag," Bill explained.

"Why would he want to go back?" Al asked.

"To get a full swing with a longer club," Bill explained. "These short wedge shots are very difficult," he added.

Ralph moved closer to the water and joked about using his driver rather than a wedge. "Be careful. There is an out of bounds behind the green. Don't hit it too long," Al cautioned.

With that advice fresh in his mind, Ralph proceeded to hit the ball in the water again. Al was frustrated not knowing how to coach Ralph. He looked at Bill and said, "Okay pro, what do I tell him this time?"

Bill looked at Al and said, "On the last swing you told him what not to do. You said don't hit it too long, remember?" Al nodded. "This time, tell him what you want him to do."

"Like hit it on the green?" Al asked.

"That's a positive command, but maybe he shouldn't hit it," Bill suggested.

"You mean I should tell him to Trust his Swing on this short shot too?" Al asked.

"Sure, why not?" Bill asked. "Try it," Bill suggested. "Just pick the right club for the shot. The club will do all the work if you swing it correctly." Bill added.

Ralph said in a rather calm voice, "That's why I've been having trouble with the short shots. I haven't been thinking Swing to Balance except on the tee shots."

Ralph approached the ball—took two Swing to Balance practice swings—and Al said, *"Trust your Swing, Ralph."* Crack—the ball flew over the flag and into the back bunker. There was a stunned look on Al face. "Great shot," he said with some trepidation in his voice. "You're over the water."

Jill had been standing beside my cart as Al and Bill had coached Ralph. She said, " I never thought those two would make it this far. It's great to see how an effective coaching process has pulled them together."

"That's a great observation. Have you recorded that in your manual so we can recall it tomorrow?" I said.

"I won't forget," she said and walked to her cart and drove over the bridge to the green.

Once again Bill and I watched from the fairway as Ralph entered the sand trap. By our count he was lying nine in the sand trap. Ralph tried his first sand shot and the ball stayed in the trap. We noticed Ron giving Ralph some advice before he hit the next shot. The next swing produced the same result. There was a long pause as Ron walked back to his cart and returned to give Ralph a different club. This time the ball popped out of the sand to a huge cheer from the total group.

Ralph two-putted for what appeared to be a score of fourteen. There was some commotion on the green as we watched the Chairman and Ron argue about something. It turned out Ralph had used Ron's sand wedge and the Chairman made sure they added a two-stroke penalty for using a borrowed club.

Ariel was still holding the flag and motioned back toward us to wait, before letting Tina play. They seemed to be checking the score cards and I could see Ron motioning toward Tina.

Bill looked at me and said, "They must have figured out the total group score. By my calculation Ralph made a fourteen and with the two-stroke penalty for having lost the orange ball, that's a sixteen," Bill added. "It probably will all come down to Tina." He asked, "How's she doing?"

"She hit a great tee shot then bladed the next one. I'm not sure how she stands." We turned and looked toward Tina's group. She was practicing Swing to Balance. I motioned for her to proceed. She bladed the next shot, but it stopped twenty yards from the water. That left her 120 yards to carry the green.

I looked toward the green and saw Ariel and Ron coming back to the fairway across the bridge. They were waving frantically. They arrived at my cart before Tina got to her ball, and Ron asked, "What's she lying there?"

"I'm not sure what she lying to here and don't you ask," I said. "She doesn't need any additional pressure," I cautioned. I looked at Ron and asked, "Why are you so concerned?"

"I realize now that it's a total group deal. Ariel finally explained it to me. Who's coaching Tina?" he asked.

"Tina's fine," I said. "Don't put any pressure on her. You'll only remind her of her dad, and she doesn't need that right now. Just watch. It's beyond your control."

"I feel so helpless," Ariel pleaded.

"I know. The die was cast on the range. It's too late now. Just watch," I suggested again.

From across the water came, "Come on Tina, *Trust your Swing,*" it was Al.

I looked at Ariel and said, "It's okay to encourage her with positive swing thoughts. Just tell her to *Trust her Swing.*"

"Trust your swing, Tina," Ariel yelled.

"Swing to Balance, Tina," encouraged Ron.

Tina came toward my cart and said, "It's a total group thing isn't it?" I nodded affirmatively and she said, "And it all comes down to me, doesn't it?"

"I'm not sure," I said. "Stay in the present, commit to the shot, and Swing to Balance."

"I can't get my irons airborne," she said. "I'm Swinging to Balance but it's not working."

She obviously knew that the next shot was critical and another bladed shot would go in the water. I nodded at Bill and suggested he help her.

The noise from the green continued, adding to the tension that Tina was feeling. Bill watched Tina make a practice swing with an iron and he showed her that she was coming out of her spine angle. This is a common amateur mistake as they are afraid of hitting the ground.

After three more practice swings, Tina was ready. Bill helped Tina and Mark figure the yardage and select a club. "Take enough club to clear the bank. It is better to be long than short," Bill suggested.

The flagstick was in the front of the green today making the shot very difficult, even for a pro. Tina confidently approached the ball and took two practice swings. "Swing to Balance," Mark commanded. *Crack*—the ball sailed toward the green.

"Go!" Ron yelled.

The ball hit right on the top of the bank and slowly began to roll back down the hill toward the water the same way Ralph's shot had done. Another foot and it would have been a perfect shot. Tina caught a break. Instead of rolling into the water, the ball stopped right on the edge of the water in a clump of high grass leaving a very difficult chip shot back up the bank to the elevated green, but it was on dry land.

Ariel couldn't stand it any longer and asked anxiously, "What's your score to there?"

"I'm not sure. Ask my coach," Tina said.

"That was her fifth shot," Mark confirmed as he motioned to Tina to get in the cart.

"I think I'll walk," Tina said. Ron was nearly berserk. Ariel was speechless.

Tina began to walk toward the bridge that crosses the pond. She had the club from the last shot in her hand and kept tapping it on the ground as she walked. Bill and Mark drove ahead to survey the next shot and I drove behind Tina, knowing that she needed space.

This is a tough moment for Tina. She can tell from Ariel's question that her score on this hole really matters. I'm certain she is having another flashback about her dad. Either her emotions from the past or effective coaching in the present will determine what happens next.

This is Al. When Ralph and I finished the hole, there was mass confusion on the ninth green. Ron still didn't get it. Ariel was trying to explain it to him. What a rock head! When he finally understood, he wanted to take control and go coach Tina.

I'm glad that Ralph and I ended the war on the forth hole. I now realize that Ralph has a very difficult time staying focused. It must be the leadership issue that Tom keeps mentioning.

The Chairman learned something very significant today. He was adamant that Ralph should be penalized two strokes for the borrowed club. He's covered with mud, but he's laughing about it. I'm not sure what happened on that hole, but he seems to be very concerned about what's happening to Tina right now. He's working hard to get everyone to stay focused to help Tina finish the hole and it doesn't appear to be about the money. He said he's responsible for this mess.

Bill is so relaxed. He is so calm under pressure. I guess it's the persona of a golf professional. All the professional golfers have that calmness about them. It must be the emotional learning process. I hope we learn how to be that way.

Enough for now. Let's stay in the present and support Tina.

Chapter 21
The Chip Shot

As Tina approached the other side of the bridge, the total group was shouting "Come on Tina you can do it!" Al yelled, *"Trust your swing, Tina!"* The pressure was enormous. Tina was walking with her head down, tapping the club on the ground. I sensed that her memories from high school golf were dominating her thoughts.

Once she reached the other side of the bridge, I motioned to the group to calm down. I could see Bill and Mark down at the water looking at the ball. I asked Tina, "What's going through your mind?"

"I'm scared to death," she said. She could barely talk.

"Stand here with me and let's talk about the moment," I suggested.

By now the group was silent, watching as I talked to her. I looked her in the eyes and said, "It is okay to be scared. When Bill is confronted with this kind of situation in a tournament, he is scared."

"He is?" she asked.

"Sure. Fear is a very natural emotion stored in our emotional bodies. When there is nothing to draw on to explain the situation, we draw on our emotional bank account and it is sometimes full of fear," I added.

"When you were playing high school golf, what did your father tell you to do in this situation?" I asked

"He'd tell me don't be scared. You can do it." She quivered under the load of fear.

"Then what?" I asked.

"I'd flub the chip, he'd get mad and make me practice all night," she said, almost crying in the process of relating her stored emotional feelings about this situation.

Once again I told her, "It's okay to be scared and Bill will help you with the shot." When people are told that it's okay to feel the way they feel, they will relax. We walked toward the top of the hill. Bill and Mark were waiting at the bottom of the hill. We stopped and I said, "You won't get yelled at for what happens and you have two great coaches down there to help you." Tina smiled, so I knew she was beginning to think about the present. I looked at her again and said, "This is a Simulation about business not about golf. It's the business meaning of this situation that matters, not your golf ability."

Tina was silent so I asked again, "Did you hear what I just said?" she acknowledged the comment so I said, "Go on down there and let Bill and Mark help you with that shot. You can do it."

She paused, smiled, and said confidently, "I'm ready," and walked down the hill.

It takes time to digest fear and telling people not to be scared doesn't help. I watched from the top of the hill as Tina walked down the hill toward the water. The bank in front of this green is steep and nearly twelve-feet high. From the water you cannot see the green surface. Bill and Mark were standing beside the ball. Bill knew what was happening for Tina. "Hard to think, isn't it?" he asked. "Bet you'd like to borrow a shot from me?"

"Can I?" Tina anxiously asked. "I forgot about that!" she said in an excited voice.

"You already used your shot from me. If you had saved it, I'd be glad to hit it for you," he added.

She looked at Mark and said, "Why didn't we think about that earlier?"

Bill laughed and said, "It's hard to save a shot for the end if you haven't been to the end before."

Tina thought about what Bill had just said. "That's a great way to think about it. I should write that down in my coaching manual," she said.

With that, I knew she was out of her old emotional bank account and I was confident that Bill would help her think through the shot. I needed to control the gallery. The whole group was now at the top of the hill looking down at Tina. They were anxious to see what was going to happen.

I raised my hand and quietly said, "The shot confronting Tina is one of the toughest chip shots on this golf course. Bill will help her. It will take extreme concentration on her part. I know you would like to watch, but we need to go back to the other side of the green. Your leadership role at this moment is to be quiet and let Bill do the coaching."

Al came over and whispered, "Would the right command be *Trust your Swing, Tina?*"

That's it," I said. "Have you ever watched how a pro on television practices before a tough chip shot?" I asked. Al nodded silently. "They take three-four-ten practice swings, then hit the shot. They must *Trust the Swing,*" I said to confirm his awareness.

The group wanted to watch and it was tough getting them to move to the other side of the green. I said, "I know you would like to watch, but you must pretend you are in the gallery at a major tournament and you have to stay over there behind the ropes. Tina needs to focus on what Bill is telling her." I could see Wally writing in his manual, and this time Cheryl was looking over his shoulder reading as he wrote. I laughed to myself and thought, *Wally's going to have a great story to tell us tomorrow.*

Down at the water Bill asked Mark, "What do you think Tina should do?" Mark was her coach and should be asked for his input.

Mark said, "I don't have a clue how to coach her to hit this shot. It doesn't look like Swing to Balance will work here." He anxiously added, "You'll need to tell her what to do."

Bill looked at Tina and said, "Most chip shots require a mini swing. Since a chip only goes a short way, it is easy to revert to a hit the ball mode. If a players tries to hit it, they'll either stub it or scull it over the green," he explained to Tina.

"I did both of those in high school and it always made my dad mad," Tina said.

"I did it too, and my dad would get mad so I know the feeling." Bill said as he looked at Tina and laughed, "But that's in the past. We don't want that emotion to dominate us at this moment, do we?" Bill asked.

"No!" Tina said. "So how do I Swing to Balance with the hill in the way?" she asked.

"The bank is steep. If you swing your normal swing, you will stub the club in the ground. The ball might go forward a few feet, but it will roll back down the hill into the water," Bill explained. "Let me show you what I mean." Bill dropped a ball and swung the club with his body in an upright posture. The club imbedded in the ground after it hit the ball, the ball jumped up the bank ten feet, and rolled back into the water.

"That's not what we want. Would you agree?" he asked both Mark and Tina.

"Of course not," she replied. "We need to get it on the green."

Bill then looked at Tina and said, "Let's go look at the green. If we start with the end in mind, we will determine where we want the ball to end up after this chip. Is that a good thing to do before we play the shot?" he asked.

"I guess so," she replied.

"Well, all the pros would do it that way. Let's take a look."

As they emerged at the top of the bank, the gallery was silent. The silence was an important leadership role and Bill knew that from years of playing in tough situations. The ability to focus without distractions from the gallery is critical at a moment like this. He looked at Tina and said, "In a professional tournament the pro would start with the end in mind. She would determine where she wants the ball to be after playing the shot. It's like billiards. Where do you want the cue ball to be after the shot?" he explained. "So we have a little work to do."

"There is a sand trap over the green in direct line with the flag and the ball and there is an out of bounds behind the trap." He said to Tina, "If we play the chip shot too long we'll be in that trap and have to blast out back toward the water. Do you want to do that?" he asked.

"No?" Tina said in a questioning sort of way. "Do I?" she asked.

"It depends on how confident you are in your sand game." Bill explained, "There are times when a pro would prefer to be in the sand rather than the high rough. It also depends on the lead you may have or how many shots you can afford to spend.

If we need to get it up and down in two shots, we may have to risk playing toward the sand. If we have a four-shot cushion, we may want to play away from the flag, leaving a longer putt," he suggested. "What's your cushion?"

Tina looked toward Ariel and asked what she needed to make. Ariel yelled, "You need to make a nine for us to break par."

Tina looked at Ariel and asked anxiously, "How do you know that?"

Ariel said, "Mike has it figured out. You need a nine or better!"

Bill calmly said, "You're lying five on the bank. Six on the green and two putts will give you an eight. Six on and three putts will give you a nine. If the chip goes in that sand trap, you'll have trouble making a nine. What do you think?" Bill was trying to paint the picture on the box top for her. Tina had to see her options, not just understand them.

"We have to get the chip shot on the green, and I think we should play away from the pin. I don't want to get in that trap," Tina said emphatically. "I'm horrible out of the sand and there isn't a sand wedge in this rental set."

"Okay, that will be our strategy," Bill confirmed. A lot of thinking has to go into every shot, but a shot like this requires some thought about the shot after this shot. It can't be done in an emotional state of fear or anger.

"It's okay to be a little scared." Bill paused and looked at Tina and said, "If I was going to hit this shot, I'd still be a little scared." Tina looked at Bill and once again seemed to relax in response to Bill's statement. They walked back to the ball. "Do you have the end in mind and know the strategy to get there?" Bill asked. He looked at Mark and asked, "Are you comfortable with her decision?"

Mark said, "Sounds good to me, but how does she get this chip up the hill?"

"That's the job of the club," Bill suggested.

Bill paused, and as many pros do in this situation, took several imaginary practice swings without a club in his hand. He could now visualize the shot and said, "Okay the next step is to decide how to execute the shot."

"But what if I don't get it up the hill?" Tina asked

"Don't speculate," Bill said. "The worst thing you can do is doubt your strategy before a shot. You must be committed to the shot. If the execution doesn't happen as you planned, we'll rethink the strategy at that time. We need to stay in the present and be committed to the shot. Are you clear about that?" Bill asked with some insistence in his voice.

Tina was now focused on the shot. Even the noise from the geese in the water behind her did not distract her. It's like shooting a free throw in basketball with all the waving balloons in the background. Total focus is the key to success in the present. The only thing that matters is the next shot.

Bill began to explain the execution of the chip shot swing by saying, "We want to swing the club just like the Swing to Balance method. But, in this case we only want a half swing from here to here." Bill demonstrated by saying, "From Toll Booth to Toll Booth."

We invented the mental picture of the Toll Booth just for situations like this. It is a good visual image, rather than a mechanical thought. Tina nodded her head and reached her hands backward to a perfect Toll Booth position.

"That's terrific," Bill said. "In order to swing through the Toll Booth on the forward swing, you need to tilt your body a little to the right so your spine angle is perpendicular to the slope of the ground. The bank is steep so you will have to tilt until you can swing without hitting the ground. I'll show you, then you can do it."

Bill demonstrated the tilt and the swing. "Now you try it."

Tina tried it and stubbed the club into the ground on the first try. "That's okay. What does that tell you, you need to do different the next time?" Bill asked.

"I need to tilt a little more?" she asked in her questioning tone.

"Try it," Bill suggested.

This time, it worked. "I see—that's easy. But I can't swing all the way to Balance or I'll fall backward in the water."

"Toll Booth to Toll Booth," Bill said. "You must see the Toll Booth on both sides of the swing and be committed to swing the club through the ball. Do you understand that?" Bill asked.

"Yes, I think so?" Tina replied.

"You must swing the club through the ball. You must not hit at the ball. Bill demonstrated again what he meant. He handed Tina the club and said, "Try it three or four times so it's in your muscle memory. Then we can select the right club for the shot."

Tina tilted her body and swung the club easily Toll Booth to Toll Booth four times. Bill recalled the number of hours that he had worked on this technique.

Up on the green the gallery was getting anxious. They could not see Tina practicing the swing. Someone said, "They must have fallen in." Everyone laughed to break the tension.

"Great swings!" Bill reinforced Tina for her practice swings. Bill looked at Mark and said, "Now we must select the right club to put in that swing."

Bill went through the options and showed Tina how the loft of the club should match the slope of the bank and the distance we want the ball to travel. This was very confusing for her so Bill said, "As your caddie, I think you ought to use an 8-iron."

Tina looked at Bill and asked, "Does the caddie help select the club for the pro?"

"Always. The pro has the final say, depending on the type of shot she wants to play, but she always listens to her caddie's advice," Bill suggested. He was telling her that it was her choice, but he would strongly recommend the 8-iron. She got the message when he handed her the club and said, "Here, choke down on the grip a little, swing it several times and see if it feels comfortable in that swing."

Tina tilted her body and swung the club three times. "Feels great!" she said.

"You're ready. Commit to the shot. Toll Booth to Toll Booth. *Trust your Swing, Tina,*" Bill encouraged.

Tina took two more practice swings, stepped up to the ball, tilted her body, and swung. The ball went gently up the slope of the bank and landed softly ten feet from the pin. It looked so easy.

The screaming from the gallery was deafening. Tina ran up the bank to see where the ball had landed. When she saw it on the green she pumped her fist like Tiger Woods. I restrained the gallery by saying, "It's not over. Stay behind the ropes."

Tina gave Mark a high five and confidently grabbed her putter. What an emotional state change, from terrified to ecstatic. That is the joy and reward of leadership.

When Bill reached the top of the bank, he looked at me, shook his head and smiled. He came over to me and could barely talk but said, "Keep the gallery quiet. That's a tough putt."

Tina saw Bill and raced over to give him a hug. After the hug, Bill quickly said, "It's not over. We need to stay focused." Tina could have easily begun to celebrate too soon. Bill calmly said, "You're not finished." The tension of the putt could be as big as the chip shot. We've all seen players miss short putts to lose major championships. The focus on the moment must be maintained.

Tina and Bill read the putt, practiced the stroke, and Tina rolled the ball two inches from the cup. Tina tapped in the final putt for an eight and the celebration began. Bill walked over to me and said, "Don't ever doubt Swing to Balance."

Then, from out of the group we heard Ron shout, "Where's the money?" All of a sudden the total group went silent. There was a long pause, and Al angrily said, "It's going to charity."

It seemed like an eternity, but the celebration mood quickly returned as someone yelled, "It's Miller time." The high fives continued as everyone moved to their carts and headed toward the Club House.

This is Al. You weren't there so it's hard to understand how emotionally drained we were. We were physically exhausted, but the emotional strain had taken its toll. When I told Ron the money was going to charity, we could all see his anger return. What is it about money? I'm sure he still thought the money was his.

That statement took the thrill out of the situation for me. Why couldn't we just celebrate the moment, the joy Tina was feeling about the shot. Why did we have to measure the success of the moment by money? Money has no meaning at this time.

When someone shouted, "It's Miller time!" The entire group headed toward the Club House for a beer. I was not excited.

Chapter 22
The Official Score

It was nearly 4:00. I could see a foursome in the fairway anxiously waiting for the group to clear the green. As I walked toward my cart, there stood Bill. Both of us were emotionally drained. Bill said, "Can you believe that chip shot? I gave her a 100 to 1 chance of getting the ball on the green," he said.

"Totally unbelievable. That was great coaching," I said. "We need to catch the group before they go to the bar. We have to do the official scoring yet today." We jumped in our carts and raced toward the Club House.

Everyone was emptying their personal belongings from the carts when I said, "I know you're anxious for a beer, but I would like everyone to come back to the seminar room so that we can do the official scoring." There was an obvious groan of protest. "We need to see how much money you've won, then we can celebrate," I added. "Please give your score card to Bill. Make sure it is signed," I yelled.

"Give the money to charity," someone yelled. "It's Miller time."

It was hard to corral everyone into the room. The emotional high was dominating everyone except Al. I could see that his mood was far from celebrating. "What's wrong?" I asked him.

"Why is he that way?" Al asked

"You mean Ron?" I asked.

"Why did he have to spoil the moment. It wasn't about the money. It was about Tina," Al said.

"It's about both, but you're right, he has a strong hit the numbers mentality. Record how you're feeling and we'll talk about it tomorrow. For now, let go of your anger and go celebrate with Tina," I suggested.

The room was a buzz with all the stories. Bob was telling the mud bath story. "You should have seen the look on his face when he realized it was his turn in the water," Bob laughed. "He egged us into the water only to find himself in it too."

"Sounds familiar," someone said.

"If everyone will take a seat, we need to do one important thing before we break for the day. We need to figure the final score to see how much money you've won." Once they were seated, I asked Bill to began the official scoring process and calculate the total group score.

"I thought the money goes to charity like Al said?" Sharon asked.

"We need to determine how much we can give to charity," I suggested.

"We broke par. We won $1,200," Jill said. Jill had been rather quiet all day. She seemed to have fun, but her CFO role was now going to show.

"We'll see in a moment if you're right." Bill had transferred the individual score cards to a large scoring sheet. As he taped it to the flip chart the room went silent.

Group	Hole									
	1	2	3	4	5	6	7	8	9	
	Par 4	Par 5	Par 4	Par 3	Par 4	Par 4	Par 4	Par 3	Par 5	
Ron/Ariel	(4)	6	6.2	2	3	4	5	6.2	16	
Bob/Frank	6	(4)	5	5.8	(3)	16	6	6.4	20	
Al/Ralph	6	7	6	(1)	6	4	7	(6.0)	15	
Tina/Mark	6	8.2	(2)	4	6	(3)	(3)	6.6	8	
Total Group	4	4	2	1	3	3	3	6		

"Oh, I see," someone said. The best score from any group was circled and posted on the total group line, except for the ninth hole. Some people can't visualize the 'total group' score until it is in written form.

The total group score was five under par after the eighth hole and it all depended on the score on the ninth hole as to whether they would win $400 or $1,200. Because the nongolfers could be easily confused, Bill explained the scoring hole by hole. Then he announced, "The total group is five under par through eight and you need a nine or better on the par 5 ninth hole to win all the money."

"Tina made the eight!" Ron shouted. "Mark it down. What's the big deal?"

Bill calmly looked at the group and said, "That's true if there aren't any penalty stokes unaccounted for."

Bill then calmly asked, "Ariel, do you have the original orange ball?"

There was a stunned silence and all eyes shifted to Ariel. She laughed and said, "No. I hit it in the water on the first hole."

Bill took the black marker and changed her 16 to an 18.

"What are you doing?" Ron protested. "Ariel's score doesn't matter."

"It matters that it is correct on the official score card so that your 4 on one is legitimate," Bill said calmly.

"Why are you adding two strokes to her score?" Cheryl asked.

"The rules on the ninth tee were that only the orange ball player's score counted and there was a two-stroke penalty for failure to return the orange ball to the official scorer," Bill explained. "None of the cards that were turned in included the penalty strokes. We need to be accurate before we sign the official score."

"I didn't know that," Cheryl said. "Wish we would have known that on the ninth tee." She added, "I wouldn't have let Wally play that orange ball on the ninth hole."

I thought, *The rules were clearly announced on the ninth tee but people selectively listen. They only hear what they want to hear. They heard that the orange ball player was to play the hole and failed to hear the last statement about returning the orange ball. It's the same in business.*

"That's a great observation." Bill turned to Wally and asked, "Wally, do you have the orange ball?"

"No. I hit it in the weeds on nine," he said.

Bill calmly marked out Wally's 20 and made it a 22. All of a sudden the room grew very quiet. Everyone was now aware that it would all come down to whether Tina still had the orange ball. No one was breathing. Bill asked, "Ralph, do you have the orange ball?" Once again the answer was no. Bill corrected Ralph's score from 15 to 17.

The suspense was frightening as Bill turned to Tina and calmly asked, "Tina, do you have the orange ball?"

She told Bill she had retired it on the second hole. What did that mean? I thought. The entire monetary success of the total group came down to this moment, and the room was silent.

The entire group was focused on Tina when she said, "You mean that orange thing that was supposed to bring me good luck? I retired it on the second hole. I lost it," she said.

The room was silent. What a moment!

Bill took the marker and changed the 8 for Tina's group to a 10 and recorded a 10 in the total group line.

Group	Hole									
	1	2	3	4	5	6	7	8	9	
	Par 4	Par 5	Par 4	Par 3	Par 4	Par 4	Par 4	Par 3	Par 5	
Ron/Ariel	4	6	6.2	2	3	4	5	6.2	18	
Bob/Frank	6	4	5	5.8	3	16	6	6.4	22	
Al/Ralph	6	7	6	1	6	4	7	6.0	17	
Tina/Mark	6	8.2	2	4	6	3	3	6.6	10	
Total Group	4	4	2	1	3	3	3	6	10	36

He then announced, "The official score of the Total Group is 36."

Bill looked at me in silence. The ball was in my court. I hate this moment during the Simulation. It is much better when a group wins. It is always close as it was in this case. If I remain silent, someone will speak. It takes a while to go from an emotional state to logical thinking. The first thing is generally an emotional outburst of protest and it didn't take long.

"That's robbery! You cheated us!" protested Ron.

He was about to rip us again when Al interrupted by saying, "That's not right, Ron!" Ron could tell that Al was angry. Al's anger from the ninth hole was still alive. "Tom and Bill tried to help us all day long. They gave us clues all day long. We were just blind to what was happening. We didn't have the right strategy all day. This isn't about someone cheating us. It's about —

Mark interrupted, "Al's right, Ron. If we had used the alternate shot format differently, we could have easily broken par. Look at the eighth hole. We all used the all play on that hole for some reason. That's what cost us the money. Can you all see it now?" he asked.

Wally chimed in, "I tried to tell you all that on the first tee. Total group is total group, guys! Start with the end in mind, remember?" he asserted.

"Be gentle, Wally," Al coached. "None of us realized that this morning on the range."

"I did," Wally said. "I tried to tell you guys, but nobody would listen."

It is amazing how Wally processes his awareness. It is true that he saw the importance of the total group deal on the first tee, but I distinctly remember him saying he wasn't going to tell anyone because they wouldn't listen to him. Now he wants to rub it in that they didn't listen. I'll bet that's his whacking mechanism at work, also. No wonder no one listened to him? He'll have to learn to influence effectively tomorrow, I thought.

I regained control before the blaming got out of hand by saying, "Hindsight is always twenty-twenty. It is easy to see after the fact. Let's not try to fix the blame, rather let's extract meaning from the total experience." The group had a very sober look and I was confident we could suspend Miller time for a while so I continued, "The total group has won $400. You can decide how much of that amount you want to give to charity."

"But we were so close to tripling our money," Ariel said. "All that work by Tina and we come up one shot short, and it's a penalty shot!" she exclaimed.

I remained silent for a moment and Al said, "It's not about the money guys. It's about leadership. Had we started with the end in mind we would have figured it out on the range." Al then looked at Wally and said, "Wally, you had it figured out. Why didn't you tell someone?"

Cheryl interrupted and said, "It's my fault. I ignored Wally on the range. He tried to tell all of us but we wouldn't listen. We told him he was paranoid." With that the room burst into laughter. The somber mood was over.

The laughter about Wally gave me a chance to gain control and I said, "You will all find reasons to blame yourself for what happened. Everyone will recall a way that the group could have saved a stroke or two. A strategy change on the eighth hole, a borrowed shot there, you will quickly figure out that you could have easily broken par if you knew about the ninth hole in advance."

I went on, "The same is true with Bill after any tournament. Professionals replay every round to determine what would have put them in the winner's circle. That's a very different approach from blaming the outcome on an external person or condition. That's the leadership challenge. That's why today was a business Simulation on the golf course, not a round of golf on a business day. Today was about leadership and being successful at work. Our intent was not to cheat you, Ron, but to orchestrate an experience that will have an impact on how you run your business tomorrow."

The Chairman had his hand up and was determined to talk. "I'll tell you what this means. I wasn't with you on the first day, but Al's been right for six months now. We better rethink our strategy." He paused and said, "I learned that we cheat and when we get caught we blame those who make the rules or worse yet, try to intimidate them into giving us a break. The customers are making the rules and we can't cheat and intimidate them any longer."

He had the floor and continued, "The sixth hole was a tough lesson for me, but I learned that there is no such thing as a gimme in golf." He looked at Bill and said, "Thanks Bill, I needed that." Everyone could hear the emotion in his voice. "That's why I made you add two strokes for using Ron's sand wedge, Ralph. USGA Rules are very precise." He paused and continued, "I know two other places where we cheated on that card and I'm sure every group could find a place where they violated the rules. So, it's not Tina's fault for not bringing back the orange ball."

At this moment, I could see why Frank was the Chairman. He had a very professional presence about him in defeat. His leadership ability was now showing.

"We need to learn from this experience how to appreciate the contribution of every person in our organization. I can see how every swing mattered," he said

Ron stood up and Frank went silent. "I'm sorry. I shouldn't have said that." He paused and said, "Frank, you're right. I see it now. We lose customers one orange ball player at a time. It doesn't matter how good my game is. It's the game of the orange ball players that matters." He went on, "I spent all my time on the driving range trying to prove how good a player I was. I ignored coaching Ariel. Frankly, I thought it was a waste of time." He choked for a moment and everyone could tell that this was coming from his heart not his brain.

Ron went on, "It all came down to Tina, Wally, Ralph, and Ariel. They are all beginner golfers, and I for one completely ignored them. I thought it was about the money. If I had it to do it all over again tomorrow, I wouldn't hit one ball on the range. I would make sure Ariel was prepared for that ninth hole. That's what we need to get out of this thing. How are we preparing the orange ball players at our company?" he asked. "That's the question for tomorrow."

There was silence. Everyone could feel the emotion and sincerity of Ron's question. I looked at Al to see if he was buying it.

I said, "Thanks Ron, but there's no need to apologize. That's why we're here, to experience the natural emotions of losing." I paused until I had everyone's attention and said, "And the money is important. Without the money there would have been no passion on the ninth hole. Tonight, as you rethink the entire day, I want you to think about what it would have been like if there had been no money in the Simulation."

I could see people rethinking the money already. It becomes very obvious that the money plays a major role. It motivates some and discourages others.

With that moment of silence I asked, "How many of you feel like you have orange ball players in your department?" Every hand went up.

"Every engineer in my department has the orange ball when a special comes in," Ralph suggested.

"Then they throw it to my people," said Al.

"Then they throw it back to my sales people and tell them we shouldn't play with orange balls," said Ron. "I argued with the orange ball rules on the ninth tee. You saw it, Ariel. I didn't even know there was an orange ball player and now we admit we all have them. We're all blind to the trauma that they experience every day," he added, "It must be a real burden for all of them."

"And we blindly press on thinking that *doing more with less* will be the solution," it was Jill the CFO. When she speaks everyone, even the Chairman listens. *What a bright person,* I thought. She continued, "I didn't think we should spend all this money on a golf outing. I told you that, Bob, remember?" Bob nodded. "But can you see the leverage point in this thing? We could have tripled the money with a Human Resource strategy—not a financial strategy. Doing more with less is killing our motivation and costing us people. We really need to think this thing through tomorrow," she concluded. The room was silent.

With Jill's statement about more with less, once again there was silence. The Chairman's favorite command was to do more with less. The Chairman interrupted the silence by saying, "That's what I mean by cheating. We have to change that strategy."

He looked at me and asked, "Rather than doing more with less, how should we think about our game at work? How should we say it to our people?"

I looked at him and said, "That is a great question. In golf the game itself doesn't change so you must change how you think about playing the game. You are either hitting the ball or Swinging to Balance and letting the club hit the ball. Because your clubs don't change and every shot is different, you are playing the game *different with the same.* That's what I suggest to clients who are stuck in more with less thinking."

Everyone was exhausted and we were now beginning to examine the business meaning of the Simulation, which was the agenda for tomorrow. So I said, "With that one thought about tomorrow, I would like to suggest that we defer any further intellectual processing until then. Are there any further comments about the golf experience that anyone wants to make before we celebrate?"

Tina stood up and said, "I feel bad about the orange ball, but it wouldn't have mattered without Bill's help all day long. Without his coaching, our group would not have made it to the ninth hole. We mentally quit after we saw Ron hit his tee shot on one. We figured we couldn't beat Ron and we quit and stayed. If it hadn't been for Bill's coaching, we would have gone to the Club House three hours ago."

"He was great." The chant started, "Bill, Bill, Bill!"

"With his help we were one under on five holes," Sharon added. "And four of those scores counted in the total group score."

Tina continued, "You'll never know how he helped me on that chip shot. You were all up on the green and couldn't see. I was so scared." She paused as she choked back the emotions. "You'll never know how much that coaching means to me. Thanks Bill."

Everyone applauded. I said, "We'll talk about Bill's role in the Simulation tomorrow."

Ariel wasn't going to wait until tomorrow and anxiously added, "Bill was more than a golf pro. He provided leadership." Ariel continued, "He took me aside on the ninth hole and told me not to quit even though it was emotionally painful for me. If I had quit, Ron's score on the first hole wouldn't count. We all should thank Bill for saving us," she said

The celebration mood returned and someone shouted, "It's Miller time!" There was no delaying the celebration any longer.

"See you at 8:00 a.m. sharp," I yelled as they hurried off to the bar for a beer.

The entire group left except Tina. She was standing there clutching her coaching manual to her chest. She let go with one arm and gave Bill and me a big hug. "Thanks you so much," she said.

"You're welcome," I said. "You were terrific!" Bill added.

"You and Bill have saved my marriage," she somberly said.

She went on to tell us how her husband was an avid golfer. He insisted that they play golf on her honeymoon. He tried to teach her how to swing a club, just like her father, using forceful techniques and negative feedback. "I locked up just like I did on the ninth hole," she added. "I haven't played golf with him since, but now that I know how to coach, I'm going to go home and tell him I'll play golf with him again, if I can coach him." She was in tears. "And I have a positive way to do that." She couldn't talk. The tears were overwhelming.

I gave her another hug and said, "That's great!" We stood there for a moment, then I said, "Catch up with the group. You need to go celebrate with them."

Bill stayed behind. We looked at each other in silence. "That's what it's all about. Ending the war," Bill said. Bill collapsed into a chair and said, "That was tough for me. I hate it when they lose. It's a lot more fun when they win all the money."

"They'll win in real life tomorrow for having lost today. That's the important point," I said.

I looked up and there was Al. What's up?" I asked.

"That was amazing." He couldn't say another word.

"Yes it was, and it was strategic. Maybe now you can Trust your Swing at work.

This is Al. Golf is a simple game. Leadership is a simple concept. I hope you now know that what looks simple is not easy. See you tomorrow.

Chapter 23
Leadership Installed

"Did anyone wake up in the middle of the night thinking about the Simulation?" I asked as we started the third day of the workshop.

"I did and I have a question I can't answer," Bob said.

"What's that?"

"Why is leadership so easy after the fact?" he asked.

"What do you mean by that?" I asked.

"After yesterday, it all seems so clear. It's all so simple. Start with the end in mind and develop the skills of the people. We've heard all this before. Why don't we do what we know to do?" he asked.

"You're right, our cities would be safe, people wouldn't do drugs, and we would all drive the speed limits if everyone did what they know is right. The first concept we will examine today is how to translate knowing into doing."

I paused for a moment to be sure the whole group was engaged and they weren't yet listening. It was too early for them to be focused.

Bob was insistent on having an answer. He also could tell that some people weren't listening so he said in a firm voice, "Remember what I said yesterday, that we'll get out of this what we put into it?" That got everyone's attention. "We put a lot into yesterday and we need to get this answer today. Our business is hard work, but when I look at yesterday, after the fact, it is all so simple. Why don't we do this when we know it?" This time he directed the question to the group.

That got everyone's attention and there was silence, so I explained, "In the past you knew leadership as a concept. You were taught the habits of leaders, but for some reason you did not install those habits in the muscle memory of the organization. There isn't an executive out there that doesn't know about teamwork, empowerment, partnering, and being customer focused. Many of them, just like yourselves, have initiated major change programs to embrace these principles, but the underlying intention is to hit the numbers with more determination. The mandate of doing more with less is the real command and that thought dominates the command center of everyone's brain."

I looked toward the Chairman to be sure he didn't react negatively. He was listening very intently. I continued, "It's the same in golf. The right hand will execute the command from the brain. It's either hit the ball or Swing to Balance. Many players practice long hours at hitting the ball and over time the hit the ball command becomes imbedded in the muscle memory of the body. Likewise, companies become very invested in hitting the numbers and try as they might, they can't change the imbedded muscle memory of that command."

Everyone was now very focused on what I was saying. I continued, "After yesterday, you know Swing to Balance as a concept. You translated that concept into action in a simulated way and today that concept is an active vision in you emotional bodies. You not only have knowledge about Swing to Balance, you have feelings about it. It is not until a concept becomes a vision in terms of emotions that a person or organization can choose to behave as that concept implies. In a seminar, concepts are imbedded in the knowing self, but in a Simulation, concepts are installed in the emotional body. For concepts to become habits, you must experience them emotionally."

I paused and everyone was making the connection so I concluded by saying, "That's the role of leadership in your organization, to help people have feelings and passion about a vision so that the behavior inherent in that vision can be translated into reality."

"But it seems too easy. Isn't leadership supposed to be hard work?" Bob asked.

"You're right, Bob. Leadership is simple but as you found out yesterday, it is not easy."

Bob was pulsating with thoughts from the middle of the night. He said, "I was awake all night thinking about that ninth hole. I actually figured out that we could shoot 18 if we played again today, provided the orange ball players were properly prepared. We could be very efficient if we planned the strategy on the driving range."

"Once again you're right. How a team practices together determines how they play together. Every great coach knows that. The game is won on the practice field. The orchestra leader knows that the concert will be great if the practice sessions go well. The question to be answered later today is how do the people of Galexey practice together? The driving range determined your fate yesterday," I said.

Bob was still pulsating with questions. I laughed and said, "You were awake all night." I wanted to hear other people's awareness from after the Simulation before we start to develop the strategy so I said, "Bob is correct. The total group could shoot 18 if the strategy was developed on the driving range." I turned to the flip chart and said, "Let's make a list or things so we won't forget to strategize about them later." I wrote, *Why is Leadership so easy after the fact? How to translate Vision into reality? How to practice differently at work?*

"Did anyone else have an observation from last night?" I asked again.

Ron raised his hand. He appeared poised and very different today. He said, "I was awake all night thinking about the money."

Everyone laughed but Ron quickly said, "I'm serious. Think about the bet from yesterday. On the first day, Tom told us we were betting the company. Is that right?" He looked at me for confirmation and I nodded affirmative. He continued, "We worked like dogs and made a third of what we could have made. We failed not because of our golf ability. We failed because of our thinking ability. With a little smarts we could have tripled our money. I'm always telling my guys we have to work smarter, not harder and we did just the opposite yesterday." He paused and emotionally said, "I felt like a hypocrite all night."

I quietly added, *Define working smarter, not harder* to the flip chart.

Jill chimed in, "Ron's exactly right. We blew it from an economic point of view. I for one have never seen the link between the culture of the organization and the economics. I know we need to be nice to each other, but I've never thought of culture as an antecedent for profit. Yesterday we were at war with each other all day until the ninth hole. At work we are at war with each other every day. It's the macho thing to do. This morning I see a real link between changing our culture and economics. If we had just communicated differently, we would have tripled our money. My question for the flip chart is what is the real link between the culture and the bottom line?"

Before I could say a thing Cheryl, the director of Human Resources quickly said, "I'm glad you finally understand that Jill. I've been trying to tell you that for three years now. You see everything we do in HR as an expense to be cut. Doing more with less always means cut the training budget." Her initial outburst was anger. Then she calmed down and said, "But this morning I feel just like Ron. I wouldn't call it hypocritical, but we spent a lot of money on leadership and team training, and yesterday we charged blindly into the Simulation. I for one didn't even think about using the skills that we teach every day in our management classes until it was over. I violated one of the most important leadership habits— seek first to understand—with Wally. Had I tried to understand Wally, we would have understood that it was a total group deal on the driving range. Why do we do that?" she asked. "We're all guilty!"

I turned again to the flip chart and wrote, *What's the link between culture and economics?* and *Why don't we use what we teach?* I turned and said, "Cheryl, that's why golf and leadership are the two most overtaught underlearned games. Both are dependent on the experiential nature of how the games are learned, and much of what needs to be learned is muscle memory and emotional."

I paused and could see that I had everyone's attention so I continued, "Think of the word habit. What is a habit and how is it developed? We'll examine this issue in some detail later, but it takes twenty-one days to convert a concept into a habit. After twenty-one days, the behavior is installed in your muscle memory. Sitting in a leadership program for three days will not develop the habits of leadership."

I added, *Develop the habits of leadership* to the list.

"Are we going to talk more about that later today?" Bob asked.

"You bet. That's why were here for a third day," I said. "We need to understand the plight of the orange ball players and the role of leadership in helping them succeed. We all have the orange ball at times, and when we do, we need leadership."

It was still early and I wanted others to express their thoughts from last night. I asked again, "Are there other observations from the middle of the night?"

"I have an observation from the middle of the night," Al replied. "We all know that the pros Swing to Balance. We know the habits of leadership. We know that leadership is essential to our success. We know that new employees in our company struggle with simple assignments and that they lack training. We know all this stuff and don't do anything about it." He paused and said, "I feel exactly like Ron and Cheryl. I ignored the Swing to Balance thing in real life and tried to practice my old swing harder to make it work. I went to a pro who I thought could help me fix my swing. I kept practicing a bad swing thinking it would become a good swing if I practiced it long enough." He paused and looked at me and said, "You practiced with the wrong clubs for ten years before Bill told you your clubs were wrong. What is the skill that let's us know that we can't extend something that is wrong forward with more effort or more determination and arrive at what is right? Does that make any sense?" Al asked.

Before I could comment he continued, "Yesterday I started out fighting with Ralph. I brought my baggage along from years of fighting with Ralph at work. Nothing changed until I decided to stop the war and try something different. We're all at war at work. I had to let go and decide to try Swing to Balance on the range last October. I had to listen to Tom and Bill. I had to make a decision to change my game or nothing would change."

Al still had the floor, "Ron, you came to the range with your game. You were determined to play your game, and your attitude created conflict and animosity for all of us. We all knew we couldn't beat you and we were tense and frustrated on the range and on the first tee. After we saw you drive the first green, some of us mentally quit. Tina said her group almost went to the Club House early. Ralph was convinced that playing was useless because we couldn't beat you. Why did we think we were competing?"

There was no stopping him. He had to get it off his chest. Al continued, "Six months ago, Tom told me something I'll never forget. He said, if we learn to Swing to Balance at work we will work in a relaxed way. That would change our culture, Jill, and it would pay off big time." Al looked at me and asked, "Isn't that what you told me?" I nodded affirmatively. He went on, "Think about how Bill worked with us. He was relaxed all day. Professionals always appear relaxed. I want to know how they do that. If we can't relax at work, I'm not going to be here much longer." Al paused and quickly added, "And don't anyone tell me, *If I can't stand the heat, get out of the kitchen.*"

"Wow! You must have been awake all night like Ron," I confirmed.

"I was!" Al emphatically said. "This is the crux of the problem we're having at Galexey. We have to get rid of the conflict between Sales and Operations and Customer Service. We can't function with conflict. We just aren't willing to stop playing our old game and play the right game! What's the new game and when are we going to start?"

"The new game is called Swing to Balance, and you all started yesterday," I suggested. "Let me give you the short answer right now so that you aren't frustrated. The issue is one of trust." I looked at Al and asked, "Remember when I asked you to record every time you trusted or didn't trust during a week?"

"Yeah, I didn't have much under the trust column," Al asserted.

"That's right. We need to start with what creates trust at Galexey and I promise we will get to that issue." I added **Create trust** to the flip chart.

Until now Bill had been silent knowing the process of reflection was important. When the issue of trust surfaced he said, "In professional golf, all the players are committed to play by the rules. We trust that each player is committed to play by the rules, even when no one is watching. If a player cheats, he can't be on tour. The total integrity of the game depends on this single issue."

The Chairman cleared his throat and said, "I cheated yesterday. I took a gimme putt and argued with Bill about the rules. That made me think about the integrity of our company last night. Bill's right. We need to trust that others aren't cutting corners just to make things easier for their department to win. That's all I want to say right now, but when we get to this issue later today, I'll give you my opinion on what we need to do to close the integrity gap in our company."

The Chairman's comment seemed to place fear in some people. I could now see some reluctance to speak. I asked again for observations from last night and Brad the attorney raised his hand. "You knew what was going to happen to us on the golf course on Monday. You knew on the driving range that you were going to put an orange ball in someone's hand. You knew that the rules were going to change on the second and ninth holes. You knew all this. Why didn't you just tell us? It seems to me, you set us up for the kill," Brad said. "In a court of law, I would call that premeditated murder and you'd get the death penalty," he added.

"What a great observation, Brad. You're right. It was all premeditated. Leaders must always be proactive. The only thing I would disagree with you on is our motive. You all didn't die. It was not our motive for you to lose. Bill was crushed after you went to the bar because the total group lost. We would have much preferred that you won," I said.

"Yeah, but we lost. Why didn't you just tell us in advance? You would have spared us the agony of the ninth hole," he argued.

Lawyers are so good at analyzing the situation after the fact, I thought.

Tina quickly came to my defense by saying, "If we would have known, we wouldn't have learned the lessons," With passion in her voice she continued, "I'll never forget that ninth hole. I know now what my dad was trying to tell me 20 years ago. He was telling me and I didn't listen." She added, "If they had told us, we wouldn't have listened."

"It's like our customers," Ariel added. "They're telling us the rules of the new game every day and we aren't listening to them. When we lose a good customer, we know why. We don't accept their simple requests. My people get pulverized every day by the anger of late deliveries and incomplete orders. We think customers are stupid. Someone said the other day, "They'll come crawling back.—We're arrogant in our own righteousness.—I'm tired of the legal perspective. It's so right and wrong. Customer service isn't that way," Ariel adamantly asserted.

"Yeah, customers don't care who has the orange ball. They expect answers from beginners. I think we need to learn what Swing to Balance really means in our business," Wally added.

I had to stop the onslaught at Brad. I said, "Let's not pile on Brad. He asked a great question, and Brad, I think you can feel the emotion that now exists about this issue."

"Listen to the answer to this question and see if it makes sense why I didn't tell you about the end result of the Simulation in advance." I turned to Ron and asked, "Ron, had you known all about the Simulation in advance, what would you have done differently on the driving range?"

Ron thought for a moment then said, "You want the truth?"

"Sure. One of the items on our Learn To list is *Learn to tell the truth,*" I said.

"I wouldn't have been on the driving range," he said. "I wouldn't have been here. I'd have done what Rene did, find a convenient reason not to be here." With that statement he knew he hit a tender nerve with Bob and the Chairman. He quickly continued, "To me it would be a waste of time. I like to play golf and the Simulation was not golf. It was fun and games and I hate wasting time playing games, especially with nongolfers. That's the truth!" he asserted. "Sorry. Don't be offended, but I would have found something else to do."

"What if Bob had told you that you had to attend?" I asked.

"I would have found some urgent customer request that would keep me from attending. It's just like that other leadership course HR conducted. I didn't go to it. And if there hadn't been golf associated with this workshop, I would have found a convenient reason not to be here. Rene hates golf and she didn't come."

There was silence. Ron still had the floor and I could tell he wasn't finished. "I get jerked around by Engineering and Manufacturing every day. Do you think I'm going to some HR deal to get myself fixed? Fix them! Then come see me!" He added, "I'm not the problem."

I could see smoke coming from Al's ears. Ralph was about to throw a water glass at him when he said the magic word, "BUT!"

"But what?" I asked.

"That's all behind me after yesterday. I realize that it's a total group game. We all know that, but today we know that in a very different way," he said with some emotion in his voice.

I remained silent giving him space to tell us more. Ariel was about to jump in and I motioned to her to wait.

Ron continued, "As I said earlier, I was awake all night thinking about the money. But I was really awake thinking about what I did to Ariel all day. Last night I recalled her pain on the ninth hole. I didn't realize that I had caused it until after we finished. I can't imagine what it's like to make a sixteen on a hole and have to finish. I would have quit, but she couldn't quit because of me. She was going through hell for me, and I didn't realize it."

I now realize that Al's group and Ariel's people are going through hell for me at work and I don't feel their pain." He paused again. "We're putting our orange ball players through hell and we have to stop being righteous about our own justification. We have to start feeling what it feels like for them and decide what to do about it right now."

Ron received a standing ovation from the total group. After everyone stopped clapping, I asked Ron, "Would you say that what you learned yesterday is important for everyone to learn?"

He looked at me in a strange way and said, "It isn't optional."

"Could you have learned it with out experiencing it?" I asked.

Ron thought for a moment, then said, "No. You have to go through it to understand it."

I nodded and asked, "Then how are you going to teach your sales people about this?"

Ron was silent. He couldn't respond. I said, "Ron, we see sales people making sales calls every day trying to hit their quota. They spend the entire day telling customers about their game and how good it is. They hit the orange ball in the water on the first call and don't realize what they've done." I paused a moment so the connection from the Simulation would connect to his real world. "Customers aren't lost by a company after they buy. Customers arc lost before they are ever in play by sales people who are programmed to hit the numbers. Does that make sense now?" I asked.

"Is that why you didn't respond to our Request for Proposal on sales training? he asked.

"Yes, and you and I can talk about that later, okay?" I asked. He nodded.

Ralph raised his hand and said, "We all lose customers, just in different ways. We lose customers by designing products they don't want. There are days we engineer things that don't matter to anyone other than ourselves. It's like yesterday. I didn't even realize the ball I was playing was orange."

Everyone laughed. "That's typical of your whole department," someone yelled.

"It's typical of the whole company," Ralph said. "We're not focused on the customer. We've trying to hit the numbers."

Tina raised her hand. "Yes Tina. What's your view on all this?" I asked.

"Yesterday on the ninth hole, Bill said something that I wrote down last night. It made sense to me then and I think it's the answer to what were looking for now. Bill said, you can't start with the end in mind if you haven't been to the end before. I think that's it. Is that right Bill?" she asked.

"That's close," Bill said. "I practice making putts every day to win the US Open even though I have never played in the US Open, yet." He paused, then added, "You have to simulate the emotional experience of the US Open. Putting is putting unless you change the emotional experience while putting. When I get to that final putt to win the US Open some day, I want that positive emotional experience to be in my emotional bank account," he said confidently. "That's how the pro's do it. It's all done in the form of a vision. You have to see yourself holding the trophy."

Tina asked, "How can we have a vision and the emotional feelings Bill is talking about when some of us have never been out to see a customer? Am I confused or does that make sense?" she asked.

"It's that vision thing, isn't it?" Ariel asked. "I get it." She paused and continued, "The end of our journey is not the US Open trophy, like Bill. It's a satisfied customer. Actually it's bigger than that. It's a loyal customer. We all know that. It's what we know and don't do, as Al suggested. We've been talking about customer loyalty for years. The orange ball is simply a customer. The purpose of the game is to put the ball in the hole. That's where it wants to go. It wants to go there in the least number of strokes possible. It's simple folks! But we're caught up in the war. We argue with ourselves about who has control of the game. I became a stupid raker because I thought Ron was the best caretaker of the ball. Little did I know that I was going to have to take care of a customer in the end, and I'm the manager of Customer Service—no, Customer Loyalty." There was silence in the room.

She began yelling at everyone to make sure they understood her point. "And the problem isn't Ron." She paused, choking back the emotions, "It's me." The silence continued giving her time to connect to her logical mind. "Think about it folks. I'm the one who came here with all the excuses—I don't play golf! I hate golf! Ron didn't coach me!—. That's all a defense mechanism preventing me from learning the new game. I'm the one who needs to take responsibility for my own condition. I'm the one who needs to know that it isn't optional as Ron said.

I'm the one who hit the orange ball in the water without thinking about the meaning of the orange ball. It was a customer that I hit in the water and I thought nothing of it." She paused, took a deep breath and said, "Taking responsibility for the total group is what it is that we need to make happen, Bob."

She still had the floor. You could hear a pin drop. She said in a determined way, "Ron, I'm sorry I let you act like a jerk. It's as much my fault as yours. Remember when I took the club out of your hand on the ninth hole?" Ron nodded. "That was me not letting you be a jerk. That was me committed to finishing a special order for a customer that took sixteen strokes. Don't you get it? If we don't finish the specials, the whole company will fail. Don't you get it?" she pleaded.

By now she was emotionally drained. When people get it, it is very emotional, not logical. The logic of it is simple. You must get it emotionally to really understand it.

I looked around the room. There was silence. That was a good sign. The heart feels; the brain calculates. No one was calculating anything at this moment. They were all feeling Ariel's message. That's emotional learning in its finest hour.

I broke the silence by saying, "Let's give Ariel a hand." Everyone stood and clapped. It was a very emotional thing. It was Bill and my reward for the entire Simulation.

After everyone stopped clapping the Chairman said, "I think we're ready to scrap doing more with less. We need to develop a Swing to Balance strategy for Galexey."

With that I said, "Let's take a break and when you come back we'll start on the strategy."

This is Al. That was the most powerful day of my business life. We were ready to learn in the emotional realm. I could never believe that Ron would admit that he was the problem or that Ariel would see herself as the problem. The Ron and Ariel and Al and Ralph wars were finally over. We were blinded by the blame.

When we reconvened, the first question was about Rene. Someone asked why she wasn't here and the Chairman confirmed that she was being transferred to another company owned by Galexey Industries. Her promotion had not been finalized, but that's why she had not attended Swing to Balance.

The next thing that happened was Wally reading his diary. He had been up all night and had converted his notes into a story. It contained the strategy. It was so simple. It revealed the need to enroll those who were not here in Swing to Balance. How do we get them to see it as clearly as we do, now that we have been through the Simulation? It is beyond the logical learning ability of any person to understand the lessons learned in the emotional plane.

Many of us took away personal meaning from the Simulation. You can only imagine the trauma of the ninth hole. Wow! What an experience! That's why you must provide leadership for your children as they prepare to play the game of life. It is the emotional bond developed on the driving range that gets them through it. It's not a question of whether they will be challenged by the orange ball, but are they prepared when it happens? You can't understand the emotional challenge of passing the SAT test to earn a scholarship. It is all so logical to you. Our schools should somehow simulate the experience. Since that likely won't happen, you must be there when they are preparing to play and provide the leadership they need. The key is to listen and try to feel what they feel. The skill of empathy is an important leadership skill.

Every day I recall the war I had going on with Ralph and Ron. Why? It's all gone now. At that time it seemed so logical. Looking back, it had nothing to do with logic. War is totally illogical after the fact. Imagine the end of the war and ask how it will eventually be resolved? If you are at war at work, get over it. You are responsible for taking the first step.

There are so many things going through my mind right now. The mixing of the emotional and logical is very frustrating. Once you've been on the ninth tee and had the orange ball challenge, you'll understand. Trust your Swing, daddy makes perfect sense to me now. It is that simple.

Chapter 24
Swing to Balance

It was a month later when my phone rang. "Swing to Balance, this is Tom."

"Al! What's going well?" I asked and Al said the magic words.

"You can't believe what's happening! We just finished doing those care reviews with our top accounts and did we get a snoot full."

"Who's we?" I asked

"Ariel, Ralph, Ron, and I. We're Swinging to Balance!" Al said. "Our strategy is so simple. It all changed when we changed the command from do more with less to do it different with the same. We're all relaxed, working together, and actually having fun."

It is amazing when leaders change the command. It is so simple. If you are willing to listen to the customer and adapt the factory to meet their needs, it is simple. It is not however, easy. The muscle memory of the old command is well embedded in the muscle memory of every organization.

Hi, this is Al. How do you define leadership in your company? It can be different if you learn to Swing to Balance. It will also improve your golf game. Tom always asks me what's going well? I thought you might like to know what's going well at Galexey since we changed the way we think about our game. Trust your swing.

Hi, this is Tina. It worked with my husband. We're now playing golf together regularly again. It is so much fun. At work, it is also very different with our vendors. We don't use the word vendor any more. They are our partners, but some of them still have their old games in place. If they can't let go and help us, we'll find other companies who fit into the Swing to Balance way of doing business.

Hi, this is Wally. I now know what everyone meant when they said I was paranoid. I'm very normal, but I had to change the way I communicated what I was thinking. They are listening to me in a different way. I have to do it different with the same. It's working. Some days the old Wally returns. Learn to share what you are thinking without judgment and blame. It works.

Hi, this is Jill. All I can say is release the human potential in your business and the money will triple.

Hi, this is Cheryl. I stopped seeing leadership as something to teach and realized that it was something that HR had to model. Our role in the business agenda is now strategic. We have been flooded with applications from talented people wanting to work here. I wish we could hire all that talent. It is sure being wasted in other places.

Hi, this is Ariel. We don't think about customer service any longer. It's all different when you think about what makes customers loyal.

Hi, this is Sharon. Our department is totally different. We now prototype possibilities rather than engineer specials, and anything is possible. When we realized that Swing to Balance is all of us working together and the ball is the customer, it quickly made sense that the connection from us to the customer is innovation. Golf clubs have undergone an innovative revolution and we are now doing the same. Now we are far more creative in our department.

Hi, this is Ralph. Customers don't know what they don't know, so we have to show them prototypes and possibilities. That totally changed our relationship with Ron's sales people. When we have an innovative idea or new prototype, we give it to the sales people to review with our loyal customers. I mean it is different around here.

Hi, this is Bob. I changed my command to make different happen. That gives everyone the freedom to create. There are days we don't know what different looks like, but it is fun trying to figure that out. Our vision is fast becoming a reality, and that is the CEO's leadership role.

Hi, this is the Chairman. Integrity really matters.

Hi, this is Brad. I don't care what they tell you, the law is the law and there are days I have to keep us inside the ropes. I realize that there aren't laws for some of the new things we are being asked to do. The Internet is a real challenge.

Hi, this is Mark. I learned to start every sales call differently. The old adage applies, 'The customer doesn't care how good your game is until you take time to understand their game.' It is exciting working with our loyal customers. Innovation is a fantastic offering.

Hi, this is Mike. We had to change all the rules in Accounting. Measuring share of customer is very different from measuring market share. All the old statistics that we reported to the Board every quarter are now meaningless, but they still want them.

Hi, this is Bryan. Al is much more relaxed and the team thing has taken on new meaning. When Al says, Trust your Swing, Bryan, I know that we are free to create something different. We also are involved in the innovation cycle at an early stage. Our input helps shape the final designs. That makes our factory much more responsive.

Hi, this is Kathy. You wouldn't know that I attended the Simulation from reading about it. I'm sure glad I didn't have the orange ball. My priorities have all changed. We are now planning how to connect our system directly with our loyal customers. We have a beta test under way. It is amazing what a golf outing did for us. I still hate golf.

Hi, this is Ron. Don't wait until it's too late. I was unaware of how my game at work affected other people. People work every day to make you successful. After the golf part of the workshop, I thought people were rejecting me for being a good golfer. It wasn't me personally, but my demeanor and swagger. As we processed the Simulation, it was pointed out that people love professional golfers. They are good players and they carry themselves in a professional way. It was the Learn to be humble thing. I realized it was the swagger of my Sales group that turns everyone off. They see us going to nice places to celebrate success and they don't get to go. We take all the credit for company success and give them all the blame when things don't go well. I realized it's the hit the numbers game of Sales that alienates people. With Swing to Balance, it's the whole team working together that makes a sale. Respect and trust for everyone all changed. The prototyping and innovation offering changed the game in Sales. We could not exist without our teammates in Engineering and Operations. Swing to Balance everyone. It isn't optional. By the way, I'm taking private Swing to Balance lessons from Bill since the Simulation. I'm watching how a pro handles himself. I wish I had watched Bill more carefully on the golf course that day. I was totally blind to the leadership lessons he taught.

Hi this is Tom. I hope you enjoyed the story, but more importantly I hope you can take away the answer to Bob's question, "Why is leadership so easy after the fact?" Leadership in any form is about creating alignment within the followers to achieve a worthy purpose. Alignment is an emotional bond between people that often transcends the realm of logic.

The alignment that the participants achieved by the end of the Simulation was the focus of the golf course experience. Wally recognized it on the driving range but was unable to communicate his awareness to others. The beginners were focused on learning to swing a golf club. Ron was focused on proving his own superiority. The Chairman thought the day was about golf. Others only focus was to survive another day.

Alignment is the leadership challenge of getting the total organization focused on the customer. This is such a simple concept yet many organizations today lack customer focus. As was the case with Galexey, many strategic planning sessions end with a proclamation that the organization must be customer focused and the mandate goes forth to the organization, only to be ignored in favor of doing more with less.

Alignment can not be mandated or declared into existence. Alignment is the consequence of an emotional learning experience that people share. People who are comfortable with their own game will avoid emotional learning experiences. The importance of alignment must be discovered and facilitating self-discovery is an important leadership skill.

Many people never discover the importance of alignment. Ron was a classic example. If you are leading a person like Ron, it takes great patience to tolerate the embedded muscle memory of his old game as it plays itself out in the form of arrogance, conflict, and blame. It is common for this muscle memory to exist in an entire management team. It is however, amazing how formerly adversarial people like Ariel and Ron and Al and Ralph can be quickly aligned to achieve a common purpose once an effective leader changes the context of the command. From hit the ball to Swing to Balance, and from more with less to do it different with the same are simple changes in context.

For those who think that creating alignment is a soft concept, realize that alignment is the key ingredient for economic success. At the end of the Simulation the participants realized that it would have been easy to win all the money had they only changed the way they communicated. Communication is no one person's job. It is everyone's leadership role.

We wrote this book to reveal that your tormentor on the golf course today is the muscle memory of your old game left over from yesterday. You are known for your old game. You have a handicap and your playing partners know when you are playing over your head. The same is true at work. Your game is known and your subordinates, peers or superiors know how you perform. If you are like Al and Ralph, you are sure you are right and waiting for others to change for things to improve. Try changing the command you give yourself today. Tell yourself to Swing to Balance before every shot on the golf course and before every personal interaction at work. See what happens. Let us know how it works. You'll experience the joy of "You can't believe what happened!"

Finally, we hope the story activates the leadership potential that resides within you. Take a moment to record your thoughts in the appendix. Extract meaning from the experience, and share what you learned with another person who has read the book. You are responsible for the emotional experience of your life at work and at home. You can change it today by changing the command. Leadership is easy after the fact. Trust your swing.

Hi, this is Bill. Never doubt **SWING** to **BALANCE**.

Appendix

What did you learn from reading about Al and Tina and Ariel and the entire cast of Swing to Balance. Take a moment and extract personal meaning from their experience.

Learn to trust the total group to make intelligent decision

Learn new leadership commands

Learn to tell the truth

Learn to influence effectively

Learn to learn

Learn to let-go

Learn to make choices

Learn to treat people like people

Learn to listen

Learn to be patient

Learn to keep promises

Learn to bet wisely

Learn the rules of the game before playing

Learn to be humble

Learn to link priorities to vision

Learn to under-promise and over-deliver

Learn to coach and be coachable

Learn to stay focused

Learn to accept responsibility for the total group

Learn to visualize the end result

Learn the difference between simple and easy

LEADERSHIP & G⬤LF

SWING to BALANCE

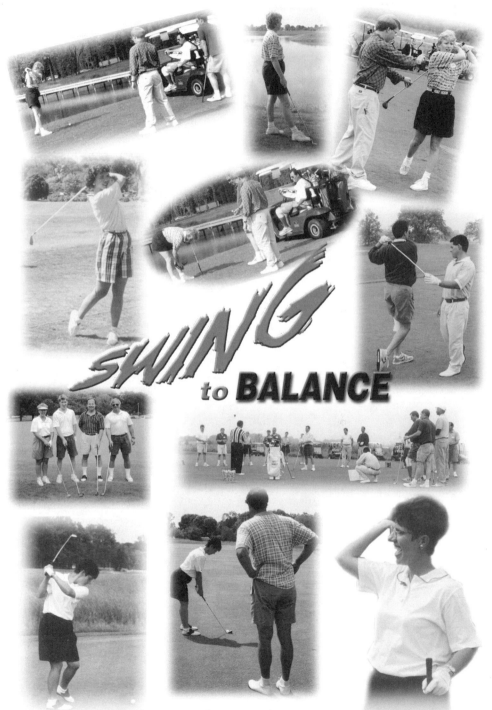

SWING to BALANCE

LEADERSHIP & GOLF

Tom Wentz is President of Corporate Performance Systems, Inc. Mr. Wentz is the author of Transformational Change: How to transform Mass Production Thinking to meet the challenge of Mass Customization. Mr. Wentz has been a transformational change consultant for numerous companies and organizations.

Bill Wentz is the Vice President, Golf Operations at Corporate Performance Systems, Inc. Bill teaches and plays golf professionally. Bill incorporates the Swing to Balance methodology into all his teaching and playing experiences.

To Order
<u>Contact</u>

Corporate Performance Systems, Inc.
5001 Pine Creek Drive
Westerville, Ohio 43081

TEL (614) 890-2799
FAX (614) 890-6760

E-Mail:

twentz@corperf.com
wentzbillstb@aol.com

www.swingtobalance.com
www.transchange.com